EXPOSITORY INSIGHTS
ON
2 CORINTHIANS 2:14 -7:4

A WORKBOOK FOR EXPOSITORY PREACHING

By David Christensen

THE REPHIDIM Project
Lifting up those who spread God's Word

Ex.17:12

The Rephidim Project
P.O. Box 145
Gorham, ME 04038

Scripture quotations not otherwise noted are taken from the NEW AMERICAN STANDARD BIBLE®, Copyright © 1960, 1962, 1963, 1968, 1971, 1972, 1973, 1975, 1977, 1995 by the Lockman Foundation.

All quotations from the Greek text are from:
Nestle, E., Nestle, E., Aland, B., Aland, K., J., Martini, C. M., & Metzger, B. M. (1993). *The Greek New Testament* (27th ed). Stuttgart: Deutsche Bibelgesellschaft.

Cover by Shirley Douglas at Douglas Design

ISBN-13: 978-0-578-58572-7
ISBN-10: 0-578-58572-3

THE
REPHIDIM
Project
www.rephidimproject.org

ACKNOWLEDGMENT

I am deeply indebted to Dr. John A. Sproule, Chairman of the New Testament and Greek Department at Grace Theological Seminary from 1976-1986, who instilled in me a love for Greek exegesis during my student days. I had the privilege of not only taking numerous classes from John but of serving as his grading assistant for two years. John welcomed me into his home and invested in my heart. He gave me a copy of *A Greek Grammar of the New Testament and Other Christian Literature* by F. Blass and A. Debrunner when I graduated. Every time I read his inscription in the front of the book, I am reminded of his investment in my life. John's passion for God's Word infected my soul with a desire to follow his example of exegetical theology. John graduated into glory in 2014, leaving behind a legacy of students like me who had been touched by his teaching. I will always treasure his input and encouragement, which has shaped my ministry.

OTHER BOOKS BY DAVID CHRISTENSEN

TRANSFORMED BY ADOPTION: The Spiritual Life of a Normal Christian, an exposition of Romans 6:1 - 8:17, The Rephidim Project, 2014.

FRIENDS WITH JESUS: Experiencing the Depths of Spiritual Intimacy, an exposition of John 13-16, The Rephidim Project, 2017.

EXPOSITORY INSIGHTS ON JOHN 13-17: A Workbook for Expository Preaching. The Rephidim Project, 2017.

THE FACES OF FORGIVENESS: Healing for the Hurts We Feel. The Rephidim Project, 2017.

TABLE OF CONTENTS

ABBREVIATIONS OF SOURCES CITED

ARCH – Archer, Gleason L. and Chirichigno, Gregory. *Old Testament Quotations in the New Testament*, Moody Press, Chicago, 1983.

ATR – Robertson, A. T. *A Grammar of the Greek New Testament in the Light of Historical Research*. Broadman Press, Nashville, Tennessee, 1934.

ATRG – Robertson, A. T. *The Glory of the Ministry: Paul's Exultation in Preaching.* Broadman Press, Nashville, Tennessee, paperback edition, 1979.

BAGD – Arndt, William F., and Gingrich, F. Wilbur. *A Greek-English Lexicon of the New Testament and Other Early Christian Literature.* Second Edition Revised and Augmented from Walter Bauer's Fifth Edition, 1958. The University of Chicago Press, 1979.

BARR – Barrett, C. K. *The Second Epistle to the Corinthians* in *Black's New Testament Commentary*, Hendrickson Publishers, 1993.

BD – Blass, F. and Debrunner, A. *A Greek Grammar of the New Testament and Other Early Christian Literature.* A translation and Revision of the ninth-tenth German edition by Robert W. Funk. The University of Chicago Press, 1961.

BKC – Walvoord, J. F. and Zuck, R. B., Dallas Theological Seminary. *The Bible Knowledge Commentary: An Exposition of the Scriptures.* Wheaton, IL: Victor Books, 1985.

BLACK – Blackaby, Henry & Richard. *Spiritual Leadership: Moving People to God's Agenda.* Revised and Expanded. B&H Publishing Group, Nashville, Tennessee, 2011.

BRUC – Bruce, F.F. *Paul: Apostle of the Heart Set Free*, William B. Eerdmans Publishing Company, Grand Rapids, Michigan, 1977.

BUR – Burton, Ernest De Witt. *Syntax of the Moods and Tenses in New Testament Greek*, The University of Chicago Press, 1900. Kregel Publications Edition, 1976. Second Printing, 1978.

CHOW – Chow, John, "Patronage in Roman Corinth," in *Paul and Empire: Religion and Power in Roman Imperial Society*, edited by Richard Horseley. Trinity Press International, Harrisburg, Pennsylvania, 1997.

DM – Dana, H. E., and Mantey, Julius R. *A Manual Grammar of the Greek New Testament.* The Macmillan Company, 1927. Reprinted 1957.

GLEA – Gleason, Randall. "Paul's Covenantal Contrasts in 2 Corinthians 3:1-11," *Bibliotheca Sacra*, 154, Copyright 1997, Dallas Theological Seminary, Electronic Copyright, 2009, Galaxie Software.

HAN – Hanna, Robert. *A Grammatical Aid to the Greek New Testament.* Baker Book House, 1983. This edition was originally published in 1980 by the Summer Institute of Linguistics in two volumes.

HOD – Hodge, Charles. *An Exposition of the Second Epistle to the Corinthians*. Baker Book House, Grand Rapids, Michigan, Reprinted 1980.

HR – Hatch, Edwin and Redpath, Henry. *A Concordance to the Septuagint and Other Greek Versions of the Old Testament (Including the Apocryphal Books)* in three volumes. Baker Book House, Grand Rapids, Michigan, 1983.

HUGH – Hughes, Philip Edgcumbe. *Paul's Second Epistle to the Corinthians: The English Text with Introduction, Exposition and Notes*. William B. Eerdmans Publishing Company, Grand Rapids, Michigan, 1962.

LN – Louw, Johannes, P.; Nida, Eugene A. *Greek-English Dictionary of the New Testament based on Semantic Domains*, (electronic ed., of the 2nd edition). New York: United Bible Societies, 1996.

LS – *A Lexicon Abridged from Liddell and Scott's Greek-English Lexicon*. Oxford: At the Clarendon Press. Printed in Great Britain at the University Press, Oxford, 1871. Reprinted in 1980.

LXX – The Septuagint

MART – Martin, Ralph P. *2 Corinthians* in *Word Biblical Commentary*, vol. 40, David Hubbard and Glenn Barker, General Editors, Word Books Publisher, Waco, Texas, 1986.

METZ – Metzger, Bruce M. *A Textual Commentary on the Greek New Testament: A Companion Volume to the United Bible Societies' Greek New Testament, Third Edition*. On behalf of and in cooperation with the Editorial Committee of the United Bible Societies' Greek New Testament, Kurt Aland, Matthew Black, Carlo M Martini, Bruce Metzger, and Allen Wikgren. United Bible Societies, 1971. Corrected Edition, 1975.

MEY – Meyer, Heinrich August Wilhelm. *A Critical and Exegetical Hand-Book to the Epistles to the Corinthians*. Translated from the Fifth Edition of the German by William Urwick and edited by Frederick Crombie, Funk & Wagnalls, Sixth Edition, 1884. Reprinted in 1983.

MHT - Moulton, James Hope; Howard, Wilbert Francis; and Turner, Nigel. *A Grammar of New Testament Greek*. Edinburgh: T. & T. Clark, Third Edition, 1978.

MM – Moulton, James Hope and Milligan, George. *The Vocabulary of the Greek New Testament Illustrated from the Papyri and Other Non-Literary Sources*. Wm. B. Eerdmans Publishing Company. One Volume Edition, 1930. Reprinted, 1976.

MOR – Morris, Leon. *The Apostolic Preaching of the Cross*, Third Edition. William B. Eerdmans Publishing Company, Grand Rapids, Michigan, 1965.

MOU – Moule, C.F.D. *An Idiom Book of New Testament Greek*. Second Edition. Cambridge University Press, 1959; reprinted, 1979.

NASB – *New American Standard Bible*. Updated Edition by Zondervan Bible Publishers, 1999.

NIC – *The Expositor's Greek Testament*, W. Robertson Nicoll Editor. William B. Eerdmans Publishing Company, Grand Rapids, Michigan, 1980.

NIDNTT – *The New International Dictionary of New Testament Theology*. Colin Brown, General Editor. Zondervan Publishing House, 1976.

NIV – *The Holy Bible: New International Version*. Zondervan Bible Publishers, 1978.

RIEN – Rienecker, Fritz. *A Linguistic Key to the Greek New Testament*. Edited by Cleon Rogers, Jr. Regency Reference Library from Zondervan Publishing House, 1980.

TDNT – *Theological Dictionary of the New Testament*, edited by Gerhard Kittel. Translator and Editor Geoffrey W. Bromiley. Wm. B. Eerdmans Publishing Company, 1964. Eleventh Printing, 1981.

TRE – Trench, Richard Chevenix. *Synonyms of the New Testament*. Wm. B. Eerdmans Publishing Company. Ninth Edition published in London in 1880. Reprinted in 1975.

VIN – Vincent, Marvin R. *Word Studies in the New Testament*, New York: Originally Published by Charles Scribner's Sons, 1887.

WEBB – Webb, William. "What is the Unequal Yoke in 2 Corinthians 6:14?" *Bibliotheca Sacra*, 149, Dallas Theological Seminary, 1992, Electronic Copyright Galaxie Software, 2009.

WITH – Witherington, Ben III. *Conflict and Community in Corinth: A Socio-Rhetorical Commentary on 1 and 2 Corinthians*. William B. Eerdmans Publishing Company, Grand Rapids, Michigan, 1995.

WITH2 – Witherington, Ben III. *The Paul Quest: The Renewed Search for the Jew of Tarsus*. InterVarsity Press, Downers Grove, Illinois, 1998.

WOY – Woychuk, N. A. "Will We Have Bodies in Heaven?" *Bibliotheca Sacra*, 108, Dallas Theological Seminary, 1951, Electronic Copyright, Galaxie Software, 2009.

STRUCTURAL ANALYSIS

FIRST STEP: SEGMENTING THE LARGER PASSAGE

The first step in expository preaching is to segment the Bible book into sections. Each segment should be a complete unit of thought. Expository preaching is not so much verse by verse preaching as it is unit of thought preaching. Compare the paragraphing of the Nestle-Aland Greek New Testament with several English translations to determine the units of thought based on the decisions of the editors. The goal is to segment the larger passage of Scripture into units of thought. Verse by verse exposition often loses the author's main idea in the details of the text. Effective exposition strives to expose the original author's units of thought so that people can think through the passage as the biblical author intended. Each unit of thought becomes the foundation for the sermon.

SECOND STEP: DIAGRAMMING THE UNITS OF THOUGHT

A structural diagram of a unit of thought traces the arrangement of the passage by following various structural clues. The objective is to see the passage and then trace in visual form the grammatical relationships of the clauses. There are excellent tools out there that diagram sentences for the expositor giving rich grammatical information about the passage. However, the danger of these grammatical diagrams is that the expositor gets lost in the details and cannot see the preaching points. The expositor cannot see the forest for the trees. We can become so immersed in the analysis that we cannot summarize the main points. Therefore, I recommend a block diagram for preaching purposes. A block diagram blocks out the main clauses in a visual format. We want to see what the author was trying to emphasize rather than what we want to emphasize, and we want to preach a sermon not deliver a doctoral dissertation.

A block diagram helps the expositor visualize the structure of the passage, just like an electrical schematic helps an electrician visualize the wiring of a device. There are five values of block diagramming.

1) Block diagramming can be used for all genres of literature such as poetry, narrative, and prophetic forms of communication in addition to the epistles.

2) Block diagramming is simpler and takes less time than grammatical line diagramming. The busy pastor is more likely to use block diagramming and will find it more useful to gain the information needed for sermon preparation.

3) Block diagramming emphasizes the important information for preaching. Most of the information vital to sermon preparation pertains to the major clause and phrase breakdown. The many exegetical commentaries and tools available can provide more specific and technical information as needed.

4) Block diagramming is more visual than other forms of structural analysis. The goal is to diagram the entire unit of thought on one page so that the expositor can see the main preaching points. A diagram needs to be visual to be effective. It must summarize the text in a visual way so the expositor can easily see the structure of the passage. The block diagram

helps the expositor summarize the essential issues for sermon preparation quickly and efficiently.

5) Block diagramming leads easily into a sermon outline. A good sermon outline should not go beyond the first (and in some cases second) level of structure. The main preaching points are the skeleton of the sermon. A sermon that becomes more detailed than that risks losing the people because they cannot follow the complexities of detailed outlines. A block diagram visualizes the main preaching points for the expositor.

Developing a block diagram:

Purpose: To visualize the flow of thought – to picture the structure.

Use the following format for your diagram.

Copy and paste the text into a word processing document. Keep the words of the text in order as you go through the next steps. Word order is important for exposition. Use the "enter" and "tab" commands to break the passage down according to major and minor ideas. Major ideas are on the left of the page, and subordinate ideas move progressively to the right. Parallel ideas should begin in the same column as the corresponding idea.

If you are using paper and pencil instead of a computer, you should divide the paper into vertical columns. Write the words of the text in order breaking down the text into major and minor clauses with the major to the left and the minor to the right.

Distinguish between major and minor clauses.

The expositor must distinguish between the major and minor clauses in a unit of thought which is an interpretive process that is basic to structural analysis. Identify the independent clauses first. The main verbs in each sentence are the keys to identifying the independent clauses since independent clauses, containing both a subject and a predicate, can stand alone in a sentence. In the Greek text, main verbs are indicatives, imperatives, and subjunctives that are not introduced by a subordinate particle. Participles, Infinitives and any indicative that is part of a subordinate clause are not main verbs. In the English text, it is sometimes harder since many translations turn subordinate verbs into main verbs for English readers. The translations that follow a dynamic equivalence method of translating are more likely to muddy the distinction between independent and dependent clauses. Therefore, the expositor should use English translations that follow a word for word translating method more closely to avoid the confusion. Comparing multiple translations will also help the expositor determine the main verbs in each sentence.

Enter each clause or phrase on a new line in the diagram. Decide the level of importance for each clause and move it to the right or left in the diagram based on your interpretive decision. Major clauses move to the left and minor clauses to the right. Independent clauses should be to the left in the diagram and dependent clauses to the right. You will often make decisions the first time through the process that you will change later as you look more carefully at the text. Keep working with the interpretive decisions until you arrive at your schematic of the passage.

Conjunctions are the keys that unlock the structure.

Conjunctions are the hinges on which the passage swings. The conjunctions form the structural clues in the passage. There are a wide variety of such clues, and they are important to structural analysis out of proportion to their relative size. Each conjunction should start a new line in the diagram. The following is a sample (not exhaustive) list of conjunctions.

a) Coordinating (and, nor, for, but, neither/nor, either/or, both/and, not only, but also)
b) Contrasting (but, except)
c) Emphatic (truly, certainly, in fact)
d) Logical (therefore, then, wherefore, so)
e) Transitional (and, wherefore, so)
f) Subordinating (when, because, since, although, that, where)
g) Comparative (as, just as, like)

Other clues help form the block diagram.

Several other grammatical clues are also useful for block diagramming. The following is a sample of such clues.

a) Participles (generally distinguished in English by the "ing" ending of the word)
b) Infinitives (generally distinguished in English by the preposition "to")
c) Repeated words (repetition is an important visual clue)
d) Change of speaker is an important clue in conversational narrative
e) Change of subject is an important clue, particularly in narrative.

THIRD STEP: FRAMING THE MAIN POINTS OF EACH SEGMENT

The clauses on the far left in the block diagram are the main thoughts in the passage. There should be two to five important clauses in each unit of thought. The expositor should principlize these ideas as universal truths. These are the principles to be explained in contemporary terms that the listener can apply to his/her life. The main points should follow the structural diagram. These main points form the outline of the exposition. The skill of the expositor is demonstrated in his/her ability to principlize the main points of the unit of thought in language that the contemporary listener can understand and apply. The expositor seeks to exegete the world of his/her listener to find contemporary life parallels and frame the ideas in those terms. It is important that the expositor works to develop the principles and frame the message for himself and his/her audience. Audience analysis is critical for framing the message effectively. Using the outlines from another person short circuits the process of Bible exposition.

2 CORINTHIANS 2:14-17

SOUL CORROSION

Conflict corrodes the souls of spiritual leaders. The byproduct of soul corrosion is despair. Many call it "burnout." We feel this soul weariness in our ministries, and Paul felt it in his ministry.

"Now when I came to Troas for the gospel of Christ and when a door was opened for me in the Lord, I had no rest for my spirit, not finding Titus, my brother; but taking my leave of them, I went to Macedonia" (2 Cor. 2:12-13).

"For when we came to Macedonia our flesh had no rest, but we were afflicted on every side: conflicts without, fears within" (2 Cor. 7:5).

Paul uses the same expression in both verses separated by four chapters in his letter to the Corinthians. He writes, *"I had no rest"* (ἔσχηκα ἄνεσιν- ἔσχηκεν ἄνεσιν). The verbs are in a perfect tense because Paul was stressing the strain on his spirit continuing until he met Titus returning from Corinth in 2 Corinthians 7 (RIEN, p. 457). The word translated "rest" (ἄνεσιν) means relief or relaxation for his spirit (BAGD, p. 65).

Paul was so depressed that he could not even enter the door (θύρας) that the Lord had opened (ἀνεῳγμένης) for ministry in Troas. The passive voice shows that God opened the door. The perfect participle indicates that the door continued to stand open (RIEN, p.457). The pit of despondency so sapped the energy out of Paul's ministry that he couldn't even take advantage of God's opportunity for reaching people for Christ. God gave him an open door, and he walked away in despair. Churches, sadly, are littered with burned-out ministers like Paul.

Conflict had erupted in the church at Corinth. Paul had written two letters to the church - Corinthians A and B. Corinthians A (1 Cor. 5:9) is a letter we no longer have, and Corinthians B is our 1 Corinthians. Paul had followed up with a personal and very painful confrontation in which the opposition reared up to attack Paul (2 Cor. 2:1). He left Corinth in despair and wrote a third letter (Corinthians C) which we also no longer have (2 Cor. 2:3-4,9). It was a painful letter and, after sending Titus with the letter to Corinth, Paul was filled with anxiety regarding how the letter would be received (BRUC, pp. 264-279)

Paul describes his feelings in 2 Corinthians 7:5. He was pressured (θλιβόμενοι) in everything (παντὶ); battles raged outside his soul (ἔξωθεν μάχαι) meaning with other people - either enemies of the gospel or fellow Christians who criticized him. He felt terrors within his soul (ἔσωθεν φόβοι) fearing that he was a failure in ministry. Few fears are more demoralizing than feeling like all your years of hard work are going up in smoke!

If we know the dark side of ministry, Paul knew it too! But burnout need not be permanent. It wasn't for Paul! In between these two descriptions of despair is a grand parenthesis of triumph in Christ (2 Cor. 2:14-7:4). A.T. Robertson titled his exposition of these chapters "The Glory of the Ministry: Paul's Exultation in Preaching." Ministry burnout leads to the glory of the ministry when lifted from the pit of despair by God's grace.

2 CORINTHIANS 2:14-17

Now thanks be to God
14 Τῷ δὲ θεῷ χάρις

    The one who always parades us triumphantly
    τῷ πάντοτε θριαμβεύοντι ἡμᾶς

        in Christ
        ἐν τῷ Χριστῷ

    and displays the smell of the knowledge of Him
    καὶ τὴν ὀσμὴν τῆς γνώσεως αὐτοῦ φανεροῦντι

        through us
        δι' ἡμῶν

        in every space
        ἐν παντὶ τόπῳ·

    Because we are the sweet smell of Christ to God
    15 ὅτι Χριστοῦ εὐωδία ἐσμὲν τῷ θεῷ

        Among those who are being rescued
        ἐν τοῖς σῳζομένοις

        and among those who are dying
        καὶ ἐν τοῖς ἀπολλυμένοις,

            to the ones the smell of death into death
            16 οἷς μὲν ὀσμὴ ἐκ θανάτου εἰς θάνατον,
            And to the others the smell of life into life
            οἷς δὲ ὀσμὴ ἐκ ζωῆς εἰς ζωήν.

    And who is competent for the purpose of these things?
    Καὶ πρὸς ταῦτα τίς ἱκανός;

For we are not
17 οὐ γάρ ἐσμεν

    like
    ὡς

        the many who are huckstering the word of God,
        οἱ πολλοὶ καπηλεύοντες τὸν λόγον τοῦ θεοῦ,

    but as
    ἀλλ' ὡς

        from purity of motives
        ἐξ εἰλικρινείας,

    but as
    ἀλλ' ὡς

        from God
        ἐκ θεοῦ

        in the sight of God
        κατέναντι θεοῦ

        in Christ
        ἐν Χριστῷ

    we speak
    λαλοῦμεν.

PREACHING POINTS

Giving thanks to God is the antidote for discouragement in ministry. The clause about giving thanks governs the rest of the unit of thought. There are three preaching points about thanksgiving. Two participles identify how God displays us to the world. The causal particle "for" explains how we speak to the world for God. The context is God lifting Paul from his pit of despair.

Central Idea:

1. (vs. 14a)

2. (vs. 14b-16)

3. (vs. 17)

Briefly identify two contemporary life parallels to these verses.

CLP #1

CLP #2

THE PARADE OF TROPHIES

Paul erupts into a doxology (2 Cor. 2:14) when the positive report from Titus (2 Cor. 7:5-7) transforms his despair into delight. *"But thanks be to God who always leads us in triumph in Christ"* The present tense of the verb (θριαμβεύοντι) coupled with the adverb "always" (πάντοτε) expresses a truth Paul now realized. Triumphing was taking place even while despairing. The sun is always shining above the clouds.

The verb translated "leads us in triumph" is one word (θριαμβεύοντι). The word can mean "cause us to triumph" (see KJV), but the primary meaning of the word is to "lead or exhibit in a triumphal procession" (BAGD, p.363). Some argue that the latter meaning is incongruous. Paul does not picture himself as the conquered person but as a partner in the conquest (HOD, p.44). At the very least, some say, we should picture ourselves as soldiers in a Roman triumphal procession (RIEN, p. 458).

Paul is painting the picture of a Roman triumphal procession for a victorious general – an ancient ticker-tape parade. We have many descriptions of these triumphal processions in ancient literature. It was called "A Triumph." The parade began with the city officials followed by trumpeters. The spoils taken from the enemy followed by white oxen to be sacrificed came next in the parade. Then the prisoners of war were paraded in chains before the soldiers marched through the city followed by musicians and dancers celebrating the victory. Finally, the victorious general riding in his chariot arrayed in a purple toga entered the city as the honored leader (RIEN, p.457).

We, like Paul, are the prisoners of war, not the soldiers, in this triumphal procession. We are trophies of God's grace being paraded through the streets of this world (WITH, pp. 366-370). As trophies, we are in the parade not to bask in the glory of the king as soldiers but to be "Exhibit A" of the greatness of His grace. This theme of a suffering captive sets the tone for Paul's great discourse on the "glory of the ministry" in 2 Corinthians 2-7 (ATRG).

What happens to the captives? The prisoners of war are killed in the end! We, too, die to bring Christ glory! The death of the prisoners was not immediate, however. The emperors often kept prisoners of war around for years as Julius Caesar did with the Chief of Gaul (ATRG, p.40). Vercingetorix, Chief of Gaul, was killed eventually to glorify Caesar. We die eventually to glorify Christ. Until then, we live as trophies of His grace bringing glory to our King!

THE SMELL OF CHRIST

We smell of Christ. We reek of the gospel. We are either the sweet smell of expensive perfume or the rank odor of a rotting corpse depending on the response of the sniffer. Paul writes, *"We are a fragrance of Christ to God among those who are being saved and among those who are perishing; to the one an aroma from death to death, to the other an aroma from life to life. And who is adequate for these things?"* (2 Corinthians 2:15-16)

Paul draws his metaphor from the spectacle of a Roman triumphal procession. We are the prisoners being dragged through the streets as trophies of God's grace on display before the world. Wherever the victorious Christ drags us we emit *"the smell of the knowledge of Him"* (τὴν ὀσμὴν τῆς γνώσεως αὐτοῦ) before the watching crowds who treat us so rudely according to the word picture Paul is painting (2 Cor. 2:14). The aroma emanating from us could refer to the practice of scattering spices along the triumphal path, or it could refer to the stench that rises from the bodies of the prisoners themselves (WITH, p.366).

We are the fragrance of life to those who are being saved (τοῖς σῳζομένοις). The word for "smell" used here (εὐωδία) means a pleasant aroma, a delightful fragrance. The word translated "being saved" is a present tense participle in the passive voice. The rescuing is performed by someone else, namely Christ, and is a continuous ongoing process. People are being rescued as they sniff the perfume of Christ in our lives.

We are the stench of death to those who are being destroyed or ruined (τοῖς ἀπολλυμένοις). Once again, the participle is in the present tense emphasizing the ongoing aspect of the process. The form can be either middle or passive. The verb in the middle voice means to perish or die, and this is probably the force of the word as opposed to being destroyed by someone else. The word in the middle voice can mean to be lost (BAGD, p.95).

The significance of the parallel phrases *"out of life into life"* (ἐκ ζωῆς εἰς ζωήν) and *"out of death into death"* (ἐκ θανάτου εἰς θάνατον) is more difficult to determine. We could make a case that the first phrase refers to the living one (a believer) leading the dead one (an unbeliever) into life, but the parallel phrase cannot be meaningfully understood in a similar way. The best way to understand these phrases is to see them as Semitic idioms. The Hebrews expressed a superlative – really alive or really dead – by repeating the word (HUGH, pp.80-81, fn18). We are a living smell or a deathly smell to all we influence in this world.

Another analogy is possible, although we cannot be certain. The Talmud and the Mishnah refer to the Torah as medicine. The Law is a powerful drug which can be either life-giving or lethal depending on the reaction of the one receiving the drug. The life-giving or lethal nature of the Law is not intrinsic to the Law itself in Rabbinic thinking but is the result that comes from the nature of those who are touched by the Law (HUGH, p.81, fn19). Paul, with his Rabbinic training, could have also had this imagery in mind as he expressed these truths regarding the gospel.

Preaching the gospel is always effective one way or another. God's Word works to produce results in the lives of people for life or death. The smell of Christ in us will always accomplish its perfect work in others.

Who is adequate for such a calling?

NO MERCENARIES ALLOWED!

The preacher pollutes God's message when tainted by money. Paul addresses the temptation to preach God's Word with mercenary motives in 2 Corinthians 2:17. Many (οἱ πολλοί), not just a few, in his day, were huckstering God's Word and the same is true – if not truer – in our day. Money motives can quickly corrupt our preaching. We can get caught up in salary comparisons to the point that we compromise our message. The goal of prosperity dilutes the power of the message.

The word translated "peddling" (καπηλεύοντες) means to merchandise God's Word for a profit (RIEN, p.458). The word carried a distinctly negative connotation in Paul's day although the noun form merely referred to a retailer. The noun was used in the Septuagint for wine merchants who watered down the wine for greater profits (Isaiah 1:22). It was also used by philosophers like Plato to describe the sophists who marketed their teaching for the money. The word became synonymous with deceitful hawking of merchandise for unfair profits – profiteering (TDNT, 3:603).

The prophet Zechariah foresaw the day when "there will no longer be a Canaanite" in the Temple (Zechariah 14:21). The word "Canaanite" referred to the traders or merchants from Phoenicia who sold their wares in the Fish Gate and controlled the financial exchanges at the Temple (TDNT, 3:603). Jesus undoubtedly saw the same huckstering in the Temple in His day, which led to His cleansing of the "robber's den" (Matthew 21:12-13). He drove them out with a whip. No room for mercenaries in the ministry!

How should we preach God's Word? We should preach out of sincere motives (εἰλικρινείας). The word means unmixed or pure (BAGD, p.222). Paul spoke about the unleavened bread of sincerity (εἰλικρινείας) and truth in contrast to the leaven of sin that corrupts the church (1 Corinthians 5:8). We must not water down the message or mix the Word with sinful desires to make us more successful in ministry.

The etymology of the word εἰλικρινείας is interesting. It comes from two words, εἴλη and κρίνω. The second word means to judge, but the derivation of the first word is questionable. It could mean "light of the sun" so the light/heat of the sun judges us by melting the covering (presumably wax that hid cracks in pottery) that hides our motives (TDNT, 2:397). However, the derivation of εἴλη is uncertain (MHT, 2:273). Sincerity emphasizes the sense of being tested or judged since κρίνω is foundational to the meaning, but we should not press the analogy to the sun very hard.

God tests our motives in preaching. We speak (λαλοῦμεν) "in the sight of God" (κατέναντι Θεοῦ). Literally, the adverb means "opposite" God although the figurative meaning "in the sight of" expresses the sense well (BAGD, p.421). When we preach God's Word, we stand, as it were, opposite the tribunal of God. We stand before the judicial bench of our sovereign judge. The warning is stark. He sees through our mixed motives.

No mercenaries allowed!

2 CORINTHIANS 3:1-18

2 CORINTHIANS 3:1-6

Are we starting over to recommend ourselves?
Ἀρχόμεθα πάλιν ἑαυτοὺς συνιστάνειν;
Or do we not need, as some, introductory letters of recommendation to you or from you?
ἢ μὴ χρῄζομεν ὥς τινες συστατικῶν ἐπιστολῶν πρὸς ὑμᾶς ἢ ἐξ ὑμῶν;
  You, yourselves, are our letter,
  2 ἡ ἐπιστολὴ ἡμῶν ὑμεῖς ἐστε,
    Having been inscribed in our hearts,
    ἐγγεγραμμένη ἐν ταῖς καρδίαις ἡμῶν,
    being understood
    γινωσκομένη
    and being read aloud by all men,
    καὶ ἀναγινωσκομένη ὑπὸ πάντων ἀνθρώπων,
    being displayed
    3 φανερούμενοι
      that you are a letter of Christ
      ὅτι ἐστὲ ἐπιστολὴ Χριστοῦ
        having been served by us
        διακονηθεῖσα ὑφ' ἡμῶν,
        having been inscribed
        ἐγγεγραμμένη
          not with ink but by the Spirit of the Living God,
          οὐ μέλανι ἀλλὰ πνεύματι θεοῦ ζῶντος,
          not on tablets of stone but on tablets of fleshly hearts.
          οὐκ ἐν πλαξὶν λιθίναις ἀλλ' ἐν πλαξὶν καρδίαις σαρκίναις.
  And we have such a kind of confidence
  4 Πεποίθησιν δὲ τοιαύτην ἔχομεν
    through Christ
    διὰ τοῦ Χριστοῦ
    to God.
    πρὸς τὸν θεόν.
      Not that we are competent by ourselves
      5 οὐχ ὅτι ἀφ' ἑαυτῶν ἱκανοί ἐσμεν
        To count anything as out of ourselves,
        λογίσασθαί τι ὡς ἐξ ἑαυτῶν,
      but our competence (is) out of God,
      ἀλλ' ἡ ἱκανότης ἡμῶν ἐκ τοῦ θεοῦ,
        who also made us competent servants of the new covenant
        6 ὃς καὶ ἱκάνωσεν ἡμᾶς διακόνους καινῆς διαθήκης,
          not of a letter but of the Spirit
          οὐ γράμματος ἀλλὰ πνεύματος·
            for the letter kills, but the Spirit makes alive.
            τὸ γὰρ γράμμα ἀποκτέννει, τὸ δὲ πνεῦμα ζῳοποιεῖ.

PREACHING POINTS

The central idea should focus on our credentialing for ministry in verse 1. There are two preaching points. The first deals with the letters of reference God cares about, and the second focuses on what gives us confidence that we are competent to serve God. Our core competency in ministry (vs.4-5) is God's answer to the inadequacy question from 2:16 since the same Greek word is used.

Central Idea:

1. (vs. 2-3)

2. (vs. 4-6)

Briefly identify two contemporary life parallels to these verses.

CLP #1

CLP #2

CONFIRMATION IN MINISTRY

How do we make it in ministry when others attack us and hard times overwhelm us? When conflicts erupt, and critics arise, who replenishes our broken hearts? How do we stay faithful under fire? Paul wrestled with those questions as the waters of despair threatened to engulf him (2 Cor. 2:13 & 7:4). God comforted Paul with the positive report of their love for him (2 Cor. 7:6-7).

People! Changed lives! Heart memories! Paul says people are our *"letters of recommendation"* (2 Cor. 3:1). The expression "recommendation letters" (συστατικῶν ἐπιστολῶν), was a technical term for a common practice in the ancient world. An influential person would write a letter on behalf of someone else. Such letters were a form of credentialing. The recommended person would carry the letter with him to validate his request for help, hospitality, acceptance, or employment (WITH, p. 377).

Paul writes to the Corinthians, *"You, yourselves* (ὑμεῖς ἐστε) *are our letter!"* The pronoun is emphatic. People were his letter of recommendation, *"having been written"* (ἐγγεγραμμένη) on his heart. The verb is a perfect passive participle indicating the writing took place in the past with ongoing results in the present. The hand moving the stylus to write this letter on his heart was Christ himself because they were Christ's letter (v.3 ἐπιστολὴ Χριστοῦ, subjective genitive). He changed their hearts and wrote their story on Paul's heart.

Does Paul say they were written on "our" (ἡμῶν) hearts or that he was written on their ("your" - ὑμῶν) hearts? The best manuscript evidence reads "our" (ἡμῶν) hearts (METZ, p.577). Paul carries the letter of recommendation wherever he travels like a man carrying a papyrus to authenticate his credentials (RIEN, p.459). He later writes that they were in his heart to live and die together (2 Cor. 7:3) - a beautiful expression of the Christian bond.

Paul's credentials were people, not paper, and they were written on his heart (and perhaps much-maligned Timothy's heart as well since the pronoun is plural). The letters were written (v.3) not with "ink" (μέλανι) on "stone tablets" (πλαξὶν λιθίναις) - a mixed metaphor - but with the "Spirit of the Living God" on "fleshy heart tablets (πλαξὶν καρδίαις σαρκίναις). The ending ιναις as opposed to ικος on the word "fleshly" (σαρκίναις) indicates the raw material used for writing rather than an ethical description of the writing (MHT, 2:378). Human hearts are the paper on which God writes his greatest masterpieces!

Everywhere Paul goes, their letters are being known (γινωσκομένη) and being read (ἀναγινωσκομένη). The verbs are present tense participles indicating a continuous and repeated reading "by all men" (ὑπὸ πάντων ἀνθρώπων). Paul's heart is an open book for others to read the stories of God's grace written in human lives.

How does God confirm our confidence to "keep on keeping on" in the face of conflict and disappointment? God confirms our confidence as we remember the lives of those He has changed through us. God uses His people, and our good memories of people, to replenish our discouraged hearts for His work.

Lord, remind me of your converts when I am tempted to obsess about my critics!

IN NEED OF CONFIDENCE

Paul has raised the matter of our sufficiency to carry out Christ's ministry. *"Who is sufficient (ἱκανός) for these things?"* (2 Cor. 2:16). Where do we find our worthiness in ministry? When the task looms large, and our need is great, where do we turn for confidence that we can accomplish the mission? What qualifies us for ministry?

Three times in 2 Corinthians 3:4-6, Paul uses variants of the word translated "adequate, sufficient or worthy" (ἱκανός) to answer his question. The adjective was primarily used in reference to a numerical quantity being large enough to meet a need which, by extension, came to mean competent or qualified when used of people (BAGD, p.374). For example, the word was used of a large quantity of wheat sufficient to meet the tax requirements. The neuter form of the adjective was commonly used for posting bail as security in a legal case (MM, p.302). Sufficient to meet a need easily shifts into sufficient to undertake a task as Paul uses it here.

The adjective was used in the Septuagint translation of the Old Testament (LXX) to translate a Hebrew word meaning need. ἱκανός was used to describe what someone needed to alleviate hunger, perform a sacrifice, or help a friend. The word focused on the idea of need. This explains why the LXX uses ἱκανός to translate "Shaddai" the name of God. God is "El-Shaddai," the Almighty one who is sufficient for our needs! Paul follows the LXX usage when he connects our competency - adequacy - with our need. (TDNT, 3:728-729). God is sufficient to meet our insufficiency because He is "El-Shaddai."

Paul says, "we are not adequate in ourselves" (ἀφ᾽ ἑαυτῶν ἱκανοί), but our adequacy (ἱκανότης) comes from God (ἐκ τοῦ θεοῦ). Paul shifts from the adjective ἱκανοί to the noun ἱκανότης, which refers to qualification or fitness to perform a task (BAGD, p.374). The relative pronoun beginning verse 6 (ὅς) points back to God in verse 5. God made us adequate (ἱκάνωσεν) to be servants! He qualifies us to become slaves. The verb means "to make sufficient," often carrying the connotation of empowering or authorizing someone to carry out a task (BAGD, p.374).

Now we can understand Paul's words opening verse 4. *"Such confidence we have through Christ toward God."* We have (ἔχομεν) confidence. The present tense verb indicates that we have confidence continuously in ministry - an assertion Paul himself needed to remember given his previous despair! We, too, need the reminder regularly in life. The word translated "confidence" (πεποίθησιν) is in the emphatic position at the start of this whole unit of thought. The noun comes from the perfect tense form of the verb meaning to depend on, trust in, or place our confidence in someone (πείθω). The perfect tense of the verb can carry the force of "believe in" the sufficiency of God, similar to its usage in the LXX (BAGD, p.639).

We have now come full circle in Paul's thought process. We are needy. We are not competent in ourselves. We are not qualified to even be servants of God. Who is qualified for these things? Not me! Not you! Nobody. We are qualified only as we recognize our neediness and His sufficiency. We become competent in His competency. The irony of our faith is that our confidence begins with our need. Our confidence in ministry develops as we discern His sufficiency in our neediness.

LETTER VERSUS SPIRIT

We are not competent (ἱκανοί) in ourselves, Paul reminds us. Our sufficiency (ἱκανότης) comes from God (2 Cor. 3:5). The adjective (ἱκανός) was often used in the Septuagint to translate *Shaddai* – the name of God as the Sufficient One (TDNT, 3:294). The All-Sufficient God made us sufficient as servants of the new covenant (2 Cor. 3:6). The verb translated "made" comes from a root meaning to "reach with the hand" or "to attain" (TDNT, 3:293). It carries a causal sense when used with the double accusative as here. The first accusative "us" (ἡμᾶς) is followed by a predicate accusative "servants" (διακόνους). The double accusative does not need the intervening particle "as" (ὡς) because of the causative force of the verb. God causes us to be servants (MHT, 3:246).

The reference to the new covenant alludes to Jeremiah 31:31-34. God inscribes His new covenant within His people. He writes His agreement on the hearts of people, unlike the old covenant which He made at Sinai. We are servants of the promised new covenant, not the old covenant. The word "covenant" (διαθήκης) is in the genitive case. It is best to interpret the genitive here as an objective genitive (DM, p.78). The object of our service is the new covenant. We are made to carry out this new covenant.

Paul goes on to explain this new covenant with the expression, "for the letter kills, but the Spirit makes alive." This little contrasting phrase explaining the new covenant has been interpreted in at least five different ways (GLEA, pp.70-77). 1) It contrasts the literal and spiritual meanings of the text. The literal meaning of Scripture is inferior to the deeper, spiritual meaning of Scripture. 2) The phrase refers to the written text versus the Spirit as interpreter of the text. This view is sometimes called the "hermeneutical" view. The Spirit helps us interpret the written text. 3) Paul is talking about the legalistic abuse of the law as opposed to the power of the Spirit to make us alive. 4) The contrast is between the external law written on tablets of stone versus the internal law written on our hearts. The law does not change, but our ability to obey the law changes. We are now enabled by the Spirit to keep the law. 5) Paul's contrast is between the fundamental characteristics of living under the old covenant versus living under the new covenant. The old covenant (letter) kills, but the new covenant (Spirit) makes us alive.

While there are certainly some valid elements in some of the above views, the best interpretation is that Paul draws a contrast between the old and new covenants with the letter versus Spirit clause (Gleason, p.76). This view fits best with the context as Paul contrasts the old covenant (v.14) with the new covenant (v. 6) throughout these verses. The "letter" (γράμμα) that kills (v.6) cannot be legalism in general since Paul equates the "letters" (γράμμασιν) with the Ten Commandments (v.7). Paul argues in Romans 7:5-11, that sin kills us through the provocation of the law even while the law remains holy and good. Finally, the idea that the Spirit gives life fits with Ezekiel's prophecy regarding the new covenant (Ezekiel 36:26-27). God puts His life-giving Spirit in us so that we can live in accord with the glorious expectations of the new covenant. We are transformed by His Spirit into Christ's image from glory to glory (v.18)!

2 CORINTHIANS 3:7-11

Now if
7 Εἰ δὲ

    the ministry of death
    ἡ διακονία τοῦ θανάτου

        in letters having been etched on stones
        ἐν γράμμασιν ἐντετυπωμένη λίθοις

            came into existence in glory
            ἐγενήθη ἐν δόξῃ,

                so that the sons of Israel were not able to stare
                ὥστε μὴ δύνασθαι ἀτενίσαι τοὺς υἱοὺς Ἰσραὴλ

                    into the face of Moses
                    εἰς τὸ πρόσωπον Μωϋσέως

                        because of the glory of his face
                        διὰ τὴν δόξαν τοῦ προσώπου αὐτοῦ

                          which was being used up,
                          τὴν καταργουμένην,

    How will not the ministry of the Spirit be more in glory?
    8 πῶς οὐχὶ μᾶλλον ἡ διακονία τοῦ πνεύματος ἔσται ἐν δόξῃ;

For if
9 εἰ γὰρ

    Glory (was) in the ministry of condemnation
    τῇ διακονίᾳ τῆς κατακρίσεως δόξα,

    much more the ministry of righteousness overflows in glory
    πολλῷ μᾶλλον περισσεύει ἡ διακονία τῆς δικαιοσύνης δόξῃ.

        For even that which had glory has no glory
        10 καὶ γὰρ οὐ δεδόξασται τὸ δεδοξασμένον

            in this matter
            ἐν τούτῳ τῷ μέρει

                because of the glory beyond comparison
                εἵνεκεν τῆς ὑπερβαλλούσης δόξης.

11 εἰ γὰρ

    That which is being used up (came) by means of glory
    τὸ καταργούμενον διὰ δόξης,

    much more that which remains (comes) in glory.
    πολλῷ μᾶλλον τὸ μένον ἐν δόξῃ.

PREACHING POINTS

The central idea should focus on glory since some form of the word is used ten times in this unit of thought. There are three preaching points all relating in some way to what is more glorious. The first compares the ministry of death with the ministry of the Spirit. The second compares the ministry of condemnation with the ministry of righteousness. The third compares what is temporary with what is permanent.

Central Idea:

1. (vs. 7-8)

2. (vs. 9-10)

3. (vs. 11)

Briefly identify two contemporary life parallels to these verses.

CLP #1

CLP #2

HOPE IN GLORY

Dashed hopes result from false expectations leading to a sense of hopelessness. Hopelessness breeds despair. Paul understood these realities in his own life (2 Cor. 7:5-7). He has been there and done that! Ministry is hard. People let you down. Hope is the breath of life, but it must be hope that stands on the bedrock of truth if we want to stand strong when all our expectations crumble.

The choice between two glories determines whether our hope is grounded in false expectations on earth or the bedrock of eternal truth. The glory of the ministry of death (ἡ διακονία τοῦ θανάτου) and condemnation (τῆς κατακρίσεως) leads to hopelessness (2 Cor. 3:7,9). The glory of the ministry of the Spirit (ἡ διακονία τοῦ πνεύματος) and righteousness (τῆς δικαιοσύνης) leads to forever hope (2 Cor. 3:8-9). The glory we choose to pursue either leads to hope (2 Cor. 3:12) or kills our spirits (2 Cor. 3:6). The pursuit of eternal versus temporal glory will become a theme Paul develops to avoid losing heart even as our outer man decays and our earthly hopes fade (2 Cor. 4:16-18).

There is a glory in the law of God governing life on earth. Paul writes, *"If the ministry of death, in letters engraved on stones, came with glory."* The condition (εἰ) is a simple, first-class, condition indicating that it is assumed to be true or presented as true. The ministry of death came with glory (ἐν δόξῃ). Again Paul writes in verse 11 using a first-class condition, *"If that which fades away was with glory"* (διὰ δόξης). The distinction between the two prepositions (ἐν and διὰ) should not be stressed (MART, pp.64-65). The force is accompaniment, not instrumentality. The law came with glory, not by means of glory. The sense can even be adverbial or adjectival. The law was "glorious" (MOU, pp57-58).

The irony is that *"what had glory (δεδοξασμένον), in this case, has no glory (δεδόξασται) because of the glory that surpasses it"* (2 Cor. 3:10). The same verbs were used in the Septuagint translation of Exodus 34 to describe the face of Moses after coming down from Mt. Sinai, where he had received the stone tablets from the hand of God. *"Moses did not know that the skin of his face shone (δεδόξασται) because of his speaking with Him"* (Ex. 34:29, cf. 30, 35). A strong Jewish tradition taught that beams of light emanated from his face or passed through his hair as the Shekinah glory of God shone through Moses (MART, pp.63-64).

The glory of the old covenant was in part or partial. The phrase could be translated "in this case" (ἐν τούτῳ τῷ μέρει), but the better sense is that of partiality. The noun (μερίς) refers to something that is part of a whole that had been divided (BAGD, p.505). It is a share or a portion of a greater glory. God's glory partially accompanied the giving of the law on Mt. Sinai. This partial glory was no glory at all compared to the glory that surpasses it. The preposition (εἵνεκεν) means "on account of" and can even mean "until" (BD, p.116). The surpassing glory of the new covenant made the glory of the old covenant fade away. The present participle, stressing a continuous surpassing (ὑπερβαλλούσης), can refer to light so bright that it obliterates other lights (BAGD, p.840). The greater glory replaced the lesser glory so that the lesser glory became no glory.

The old covenant glory was fading away (καταργούμενον, see vs. 7, 11, 13). The verb meant to make powerless or even abolish (BAGD, p. 407). It is passive - made ineffective by something else. The old glory was being replaced. The old glory was nullified by the new glory. The new glory is a remaining (μένον) glory. The participle indicates an active and continuous glory - a glory that stays or persists. New covenant glory has staying power because it is eternal and not temporal (2 Cor. 4:17). We focus on the glory that stays. This glory will get us through the hard times we face on earth.

Paul is stressing ministry (διακονία) throughout this section (2 Cor. 3:7, 8, 9; cf. 4:1) leading to his conclusion in 2 Corinthians 3:12. *"Therefore* (οὖν) *having such a hope, we use great boldness in our speech."* Ministry will drain us. Ministry will consume us. Hope and boldness come from keeping our eyes on the forever glory of our lives with Jesus. Our boldness in ministry develops from our theology of glory!

WHAT KIND OF MINISTRY DO I HAVE?

Paul draws a strong contrast between two kinds of ministry in 2 Corinthians 3:7-9, new covenant versus old covenant ministry. The word translated "ministry" (διακονία) is used four times in these three verses. Drawn from the context of menial service like food preparation, it came to refer to the service of apostles and bishops in Acts 1:17 and 20:24 (BAGD, p.184). The word "glory" (δόξα) is used five times. The verb along with the noun is used four more times in the next two verses (10-11).

Paul is showing us that the ministry God calls us to is a glorious ministry. We must never lose sight of the glory of the ministry in the drudgery of the service. While both kinds of ministry possess glory, one is more glorious. Literally it "abounds" (περισσεύει) in glory "much more" (πολλῷ μᾶλλον). The glory of new covenant ministry exceeds the glory of old covenant ministry.

Paul describes the old covenant ministry as the "ministry of death" (τοῦ θανάτου) in verse 7 and the "ministry of condemnation" (τῆς κατακρίσεως) in verse 9. The new covenant ministry is described as the "ministry of the Spirit" (τοῦ πνεύματος) in verse 8 and the "ministry of righteousness" (δικαιοσύνης) in verse 9. All four genitives should be taken in the same way with the same force. The constructions form two sets of contrasting patterns.

ἡ διακονία τοῦ θανάτου (death)
ἡ διακονία τοῦ πνεύματος (Spirit)

τῇ διακονίᾳ τῆς κατακρίσεως (condemnation)
ἡ διακονία τῆς δικαιοσύνης (righteousness)

How should we understand the genitives in these constructions? Are they simply genitives of quality or description (BD, p.91)? If so, they describe a quality of the ministry which makes sense in the last set of two constructions but not the first set of two. The "Spirit" cannot be merely a quality of ministry because it is clear in context that this is not the human spirit but the Spirit of God (3:6, 17-18).

The genitives could be objective genitives (BD, p.90) which is the way that some commentators understand Paul. In this case, one ministry leads to death and condemnation while the other ministry leads to the Spirit and righteousness. The object of the action of ministry is condemnation or righteousness (MART, p.61). The problem arises once again with the Spirit. In what sense does the ministry lead to or produce the Spirit. It is the Spirit who gives life, and it is the letter that kills (3:6).

33

The best way to understand the genitives is that they are subjective genitives perhaps better called "genitives of origin" (BD, p.89). Meyer uses the word "medium" to bring out the force of the genitives (MEY, p.468). One ministry is the medium of death and condemnation. It is the way that death and condemnation work in our lives. The other ministry is the medium of the Spirit and righteousness. The Spirit of God is the origin of life and righteousness through the ministry of the Gospel of Christ. Gospel preaching is the way the Spirit and righteousness work through us. Our ministries are the expression of His grace and His righteousness.

Righteousness and condemnation are the legal acts of God carried out through the ministry of the Gospel. This is forensic or judicial righteousness and condemnation (MEY, p.468 fn1). Paul has just written that we are the smell of death to those who are perishing, or we are the smell of life to those who are being saved (2:15-16). God condemns sin through the ministry of the Law. There is a glory in this ministry, Paul tells us. However, God imputes righteousness through the ministry of the Gospel. There is far greater glory in this ministry, Paul stresses. When we focus on preaching the law, we are ministers of death and condemnation. When we focus on preaching grace, we are ministers of the Spirit and righteousness.

What kind of ministry do I have?

A.T. Robinson wrote:

> *It is sad to see a minister of Christ who is still at Sinai, who is still under the Old Covenant, who is still proclaiming a message of death, who has not caught the vision of love and grace and hope in the New Covenant. Paul's appeal is for men who will carry the message of the Cross, not of Sinai. Paul sees in Jesus the emancipation of the human spirit from the bondage of the law. The chill of mere formalism had frozen the life out of Judaism as it has destroyed the real power of many expressions of Christianity* (ATRG, p.76).

2 CORINTHIANS 3:12-18

Therefore, having such a hope
12 Ἔχοντες οὖν τοιαύτην ἐλπίδα
We make use of much outspokenness
πολλῇ παρρησίᾳ χρώμεθα
     and not like Moses who used to put a head covering upon his face
     13 καὶ οὐ καθάπερ Μωϋσῆς ἐτίθει κάλυμμα ἐπὶ τὸ πρόσωπον αὐτοῦ πρὸς
          So that the sons of Israel do not stare at the end of what was being used up.
          τὸ μὴ ἀτενίσαι τοὺς υἱοὺς Ἰσραὴλ εἰς τὸ τέλος τοῦ καταργουμένου.
But their minds were petrified
14 ἀλλὰ ἐπωρώθη τὰ νοήματα αὐτῶν.
     For until today's day the same head covering
     ἄχρι γὰρ τῆς σήμερον ἡμέρας τὸ αὐτὸ κάλυμμα
          upon the reading of the old covenant
          ἐπὶ τῇ ἀναγνώσει τῆς παλαιᾶς διαθήκης
       remains,
       μένει,
             not being uncovered
             μὴ ἀνακαλυπτόμενον
                because in Christ it is set aside
                ὅτι ἐν Χριστῷ καταργεῖται·
     But until today whenever Moses is read,
     15 ἀλλ' ἕως σήμερον ἡνίκα ἂν ἀναγινώσκηται Μωϋσῆς,
          a covering is laid upon their heart
          κάλυμμα ἐπὶ τὴν καρδίαν αὐτῶν κεῖται·
but whenever someone turns around to the Lord, the covering is taken away.
16 ἡνίκα δὲ ἐὰν ἐπιστρέψῃ πρὸς κύριον, περιαιρεῖται τὸ κάλυμμα.
Now the Lord is the Spirit
17 ὁ δὲ κύριος τὸ πνεῦμά ἐστιν·
     And where the Spirit of the Lord (is), (there is) liberty
     οὗ δὲ τὸ πνεῦμα κυρίου, ἐλευθερία.
Now we all,
18 ἡμεῖς δὲ πάντες
          With an uncovered face
          ἀνακεκαλυμμένῳ προσώπῳ
          seeing by reflection the glory of the Lord
          τὴν δόξαν κυρίου κατοπτριζόμενοι
are being transfigured into the same image
τὴν αὐτὴν εἰκόνα μεταμορφούμεθα
       from glory into glory
       ἀπὸ δόξης εἰς δόξαν
          just as from the Lord, the Spirit
          καθάπερ ἀπὸ κυρίου πνεύματος.

PREACHING POINTS

Paul continues his theme, begun in 3:6, about the life-giving Spirit of God as compared to the death-sentencing spirit of the law. The Spirit of God gives us wonderful gifts of His grace in these verses. There are four preaching points. First, Paul talks about hopeful boldness. Second, the Spirit brings about a change of mind and heart. Third, we experience the liberty of the Spirit. Fourth, God's Spirit progressively transforms us into the glorious image of Christ.

Central Idea:

1. (vs. 12-13)

2. (vs. 14-16)

3. (vs. 17)

4. (vs. 18)

Briefly identify two contemporary life parallels to these verses.

CLP #1

CLP #2

I CAN SEE CLEARLY NOW

Conversion is a dramatic event of spiritual transformation as God burns away the fog that shrouds our thinking. Minds once petrified can now think lucidly. Eyes once veiled can now see clearly. Paul describes conversion in Jewish terms that can be applied to all (2 Cor. 3:14-16).

He writes that *"minds were hardened"* (2 Cor. 3:14). Mental faculties (τὰ νοήματα) were dulled (ἐπωρώθη). The verb means to be petrified (BAGD, p.732). The passive voice indicates that something outside of the mind hardened it. Sin! Petrified minds are dead because of sin. Petrified minds are incapable of understanding spiritual truth.

Whenever people read Scripture, the veil remains *"not being lifted"* (μὴ ἀνακαλυπτόμενον) from their hearts (vs.14-15). Some take this as a nominative absolute, translating the phrase "it not being revealed that (the veil) is being removed in Christ" (VIN, 3:308). The phrasing is awkward, requiring words to be supplied, and nominative absolutes are not commonly used this way in the New Testament (HAN, p.318). It is better to translate it as a reference to the veil "not being lifted" from their hearts since the noun (κάλυμμα), and participle (ἀνακαλυπτόμενον) are in agreement with each other. The verb (ἀνακάλυπτω) can mean to uncover or unveil (BAGD, p.55) and will be used this way in verse 18.

The veil is removed in Christ (καταργεῖται). The verb was used earlier of the glory fading away (vs.7-11). It means to make powerless, to abolish or wipe out (BAGD, p.417). The verb is passive. The veil preventing people from seeing God's glory is wiped away by God. He nullifies the veil's power, not us. He renders powerless the sin that shrouds our hearts from seeing His glory.

When does this dramatic transformation take place? It takes place *"whenever (ἡνίκα δὲ ἐὰν) a person might turn (ἐπιστρέψῃ) to the Lord"* (v.15). In classical Greek ἡνίκα refers to a specific hour or season but becomes a general time reference when coupled with ἐὰν (BD, p.237). The verb is an Aorist active subjunctive, so the person turns himself. The word graphically pictures Moses turning to the Lord in Exodus 34 as the veil is removed whenever he faces God's glory.

When a person turns to the Lord, the veil blocking spiritual sight is taken away (v.16). The verb (περιαιρεῖται) comes from two words - περί, meaning something enveloping or around the head combined with αἴρω meaning to lift up. Some take it literally as lifting up a veil that encircles the head. However, the combination of root words is best understood as intensive meaning to take away or remove. (MHT, 2:321).

Conversion means that God regenerates minds petrified by sin and rips away the veil that blinds our hearts when we turn to the Lord. We can understand His Word when we could not understand it before. We can see His glory when all we saw before was darkness.

Lord, open our eyes to see your glory. Open the eyes of those around us to grasp your grace.

BIG "S" OR LITTLE "S"

Paul writes, *"Now the Lord is the Spirit, and where the Spirit of the Lord is, there is liberty"* (2 Cor. 3:17). Most translations capitalize "Spirit" taking it as a reference to the Holy Spirit, the third person of the Trinity. However, the word translated "spirit" (πνεῦμα) could refer to the force that animates or gives life to someone (BAGD, p.674). Is Paul saying "the Lord is a life-giving force" or "the Lord is the third person of the Trinity"?

There are four arguments for understanding "spirit" as a life-giving dynamic or power. 1) The context focuses on a contrast between the two covenants, not an explanation of the Trinity. 2) The emphasis is on the spirit as a dynamic that produces life in contrast to the letter of the Law that produces death (cf. 2 Cor. 3:6,8,17,18). 3) If Christ as Lord is equivalent to the Holy Spirit, this confuses the distinct persons of the Trinity. 4) Christ is called a "life-giving spirit" in 1 Corinthians 15:45 (HUGH, pp.115-121).

I think it best, without being dogmatic, to understand the Spirit throughout this section as the Holy Spirit (Big "S"). However, the emphasis of the passage is not on the Holy Spirit as a person but the Holy Spirit as the dynamic power from God who produces life in us who were once in bondage (MART, p.71). The Big "S" is a life-transforming force unleashed by God when we turn to the Son.

"The Lord is the Spirit" (ὁ κύριος το πνεῦμά ἐστιν). The definite article before "Lord" is an anaphoric article pointing back to "Lord" in the previous verse. The language reflects back to Yahweh in Exodus 34:34. Paul's argument in these verses is that the Spirit equals Yahweh - God in three persons (MHT, 3:174). Paul is not confusing the second and third persons of the Trinity by making the second the same as the third. Paul is stating that the Yahweh of the Old Testament is the Spirit who transforms our lives today.

"Where the Spirit of the Lord (Yahweh) is there is liberty." The veil over our hearts is removed in Christ (2 Cor. 3:14) by the power of the Spirit of Yahweh whose glory was veiled from their hearts in the Old Covenant. Paul expresses it clearly in Galatians when he writes that *"God has sent forth the Spirit of His Son into our hearts crying Abba! Father!"* (Gal. 4:6). *"It was for freedom that Christ set us free"* (Gal. 5:1). We have a direct and open relationship with Yahweh as our Father through the Son, who has set us free from the Law.

Paul goes on to write that we are being transformed (2 Cor. 3:15) by *"the Lord, the Spirit"* (ἀπὸ κυρίου πνεύματος) There are at least five different possible translations of this last clause (HUGH, p.120 fn23). However, it is best to translate it as *"by the Spirit of the Lord"* since an attributive genitive generally comes first in the word order making "Spirit" (πνεύματος) the object of the preposition not "Lord" (κυρίου) so "Lord" modifies "Spirit." (BD, p.250).

All three persons of the Godhead are involved in our transformation. The veil over our hearts is removed in Christ. God the Father is transforming us into the image of His Son by the agency of His Spirit who produces life and liberty in, through, and for us! Praise be to Yahweh from whom all blessings flow.

THE TRANSFORMATION PATH

Sanctification is a progressive process of spiritual transformation. We are *"being transformed"* (μεταμορφούμεθα), Paul writes, *"into the same image from glory to glory, just as from the Lord, the Spirit"* (2 Cor. 3:18). The verb is a present tense, passive voice indicating that the action is being done by God the Holy Spirit in a continuous manner. The transformation process is God's work done with our cooperation and is progressive through stages of development culminating in a glorious finish.

Our transformation begins at conversion. Paul writes that "we all" (ἡμεῖς πάντες) now see God's glory with an "unveiled face" (ἀνακεκαλυμμένῳ προσώπῳ). He is referring to verse 16. *"Whenever a person turns to the Lord, the veil* (κάλυμμα) *is removed."* We turn (ἐπιστρέφω) to the Lord, and He removes (περιαιρέω) the veil. We now see with an unveiled face. The verb is a perfect passive participle indicating that the lifting of the veil took place in the past with continuing results in the present (HUGH, p.117, fn17).

Our transformation progresses by beholding. The act of beholding (κατοπτριζόμενοι) is something we do continuously (present tense). We are beholding the glory of the Lord for our benefit (middle voice). The discipline of contemplation is an ongoing action with personal benefits. Contemplation of His glory explains our cooperation with His transformation.

The participle translated "beholding" can mean either 'beholding as in a mirror" or "reflecting as in a mirror." Either translation is semantically correct. Do we behold the glory that Christ reflects to us, or do we reflect the glory from Him to others? The better translation is beholding, not reflecting (HUGH, pp.118-119, fn18). Christ mirrors God's glory to us, and we are being transformed as we contemplate His glory.

The transformation in us is an internal, not external transformation. Our very essence is being transformed. This is the sense of μεταμορφόομαι (2 Cor. 3:18) as opposed to μετασχηματίζω (2 Cor. 11:14). The latter word is like transforming a vegetable garden into a flower garden while the former is like transforming a garden into a parking lot (TRE, pp. 263-267). Our very nature (μορφή) not merely our schematic (σχῆμα) is being transformed.

We are being transformed into the same (αὐτὴν) image (εἰκόνα) of the Lord that we are beholding. Our transformation is "from glory to glory" (ἀπὸ δόξης εἰς δόξαν). There are stages of our transformation process. We are being transformed from the glory of the mirror image we see into the glory of a real likeness we become from the inside out (HAN, p.319). Our progress will finally be complete when we no longer see His glory in a mirror but face to face at His coming. *"We will be like Him because we will see Him just as He is"* (1 Jn. 3:2).

2 CORINTHIANS 4:1-18

2 CORINTHIANS 4:1-6

For this reason,
Διὰ τοῦτο,

   since we have this ministry
   ἔχοντες τὴν διακονίαν ταύτην
   just as we have been shown mercy,
   καθὼς ἠλεήθημεν,
  we do not give up
  οὐκ ἐγκακοῦμεν
  but we have put aside the secret ways of disgrace,
2 ἀλλὰ ἀπειπάμεθα τὰ κρυπτὰ τῆς αἰσχύνης,

   not behaving with trickery
   μὴ περιπατοῦντες ἐν πανουργίᾳ
   nor distorting the word of God
   μηδὲ δολοῦντες τὸν λόγον τοῦ θεοῦ
   but by the transparent disclosure of the truth
   ἀλλὰ τῇ φανερώσει τῆς ἀληθείας

    recommending ourselves to every conscience of men
    συνιστάνοντες ἑαυτοὺς πρὸς πᾶσαν συνείδησιν ἀνθρώπων
    in the sight of God.
    ἐνώπιον τοῦ θεοῦ.

If now
3 εἰ δὲ

  even our gospel is covered,
  καὶ ἔστιν κεκαλυμμένον τὸ εὐαγγέλιον ἡμῶν,
  it is covered in those who are dying,
  ἐν τοῖς ἀπολλυμένοις ἐστὶν κεκαλυμμένον,

   in whose case the God of this world has blinded the minds of the disbelieving
   4 ἐν οἷς ὁ θεὸς τοῦ αἰῶνος τούτου ἐτύφλωσεν τὰ νοήματα τῶν ἀπίστων

    to not clearly see the light
    εἰς τὸ μὴ αὐγάσαι τὸν φωτισμὸν

     of the good news
     τοῦ εὐαγγελίου

      of the glory of Christ
      τῆς δόξης τοῦ Χριστοῦ,

       who is the icon of God.
       ὅς ἐστιν εἰκὼν τοῦ θεοῦ.

Not for
5 Οὐ γὰρ

  do we preach ourselves
  ἑαυτοὺς κηρύσσομεν

   but Christ Jesus as Lord,
   ἀλλὰ Ἰησοῦν Χριστὸν κύριον,
   and ourselves as our slaves on behalf of Jesus.
   ἑαυτοὺς δὲ δούλους ὑμῶν διὰ Ἰησοῦν.

Because the God
6 ὅτι ὁ θεὸς
      who said "Light shall shine out of darkness,"
      ὁ εἰπών· ἐκ σκότους φῶς λάμψει,
   the one who has shined light in our hearts
   ὃς ἔλαμψεν ἐν ταῖς καρδίαις ἡμῶν
      for the purpose of the illumination
      πρὸς φωτισμὸν
         of the knowledge
         τῆς γνώσεως
            of the glory of God
            τῆς δόξης τοῦ θεοῦ
               in the face of Jesus Christ.
               ἐν προσώπῳ [Ἰησοῦ] Χριστοῦ.

PREACHING POINTS

Transparency in ministry seems to be the overarching theme. The contrasts between secrecy and disclosure, blinded minds versus seeing the light, and the light of Christ shining in darkness all stress transparency. There are three major preaching points corresponding to these principles.

Central Idea:

1. (vs. 1-2)

2. (vs. 3-4)

3. (vs. 5-6)

Briefly identify two contemporary life parallels to these verses.

CLP #1

CLP #2

THE FOG OF DESPAIR

We can easily become discouraged in ministry. Our initiatives fail. Success appears illusory. The hearts of people grow cold. Broken promises strand us without resources. Conflicts erupt over petty differences. Harsh words corrode our spirits. Losses pile up. The way ahead becomes shrouded in the fog of despair. Paul understood all too well these realities when he wrote, "Therefore, since we have this ministry, as we received mercy, we do not lose heart" (2 Cor. 4:1).

The verb translated "we do not lose heart" (ἐγκακοῦμεν also spelled ἐνκακοῦμεν) is a present tense verb indicating a persevering refusal to lose heart. It means to become weary, tired, or to despair (BAGD, p.215). The word can mean "cowardice" (MM, p.215). The sense of the word is less about physical exhaustion and more about something being distasteful or revolting (MART, p.77). Paul does not face people in ministry with a sense of revulsion. When ministry becomes distasteful, we pull away from people. We pull back from the work. Paul says that we do not develop a distaste for the ministry. We persevere in our determination not to pull away from the work.

How do we avoid developing a distaste for ministry? Distaste for ministry grows whenever we lose sight of the glory of His grace and mercy at work in our own lives as the foundation for ministry to others. Paul says, "For this reason (Διὰ τοῦτο) we do not lose heart." The introductory clause looks forward to the next two clauses in the verse (RIEN, p. 462). We do not lose heart "since we have this ministry, as we have received mercy." The participial clause "having this ministry" (ἔχοντες τὴν διακονίαν ταύτην) is best understood as causal (DM, p.275). The possession of this (ταύτην) ministry (διακονίαν) causes us to avoid finding God's work distasteful and so pull away from His call to serve others.

The ministry Paul is talking about looks back to the ministry of the new covenant in chapter 3. We are not adequate in ourselves, but God makes us adequate as ministers of the new covenant of life, not the old covenant of death (2 Cor. 3:4-6). Our confidence comes from knowing that the "ministry of the Spirit" (ἡ διακονία τῆς πνεύματος) is glorious (2 Cor. 3:8). The source of the new covenant ministry is God. The content of the new covenant ministry is grace. The end of the new covenant ministry is glorious, so we do not despair no matter how bleak the winds might be blowing in life.

Mercy is the foundation for persevering ministry. Paul writes, "just as we have received mercy" (καθὼς ἠλεηθημεν) we do not despair. The verb is passive meaning that God shows us mercy. Grace and mercy go hand in hand. Grace refers to the sins forgiven. Mercy refers to the misery we feel because of the sins. God's removal of our misery over sin is the mercy we experience from Him (TRE, p.169). God forgives our sins, and God removes the misery of those sins. God's mercy removes our misery so we can offer His mercy to others in their misery. For this reason, we do not despair as long as we focus on the mercy God has shown us.

We do not become discouraged because His ministry energizes us as His mercy humbles us. The ministry is not dependent on us but on Him, so to despair in the ministry is to despair in God. A sense of dependency grounds our ministry in His grace. We are what we are and do what we do not by our abilities but by the power of His Spirit, which culminates in unfailing glory (2 Cor. 3:6-8). Humbled by His mercy toward us, we persevere in ministering mercy to others. Mercy removed our misery. How can we fail to offer that same mercy to others?

MINISTRY SUCCESS THROUGH HIDDEN METHODS

Pragmatism makes a poor foundation for success in ministry. Doing whatever works may produce impressive results in the short term but leads to disillusionment in the end. Ministries built on the latest marketing methods and persuasive techniques - style without substance - produce temporal, not eternal results. Paul wrote: *"We do not lose heart, but we have renounced the things hidden because of shame, not walking in craftiness or adulterating the word of God, but by the manifestation of truth commending ourselves to every man's conscience in the sight of God"* (2 Corinthians 4:2).

Paul is defending himself against his critics in the church who were impressed with the self-promotion of what he calls the "super-apostles" (2 Cor. 11:5; 12:11). These marketing wizards of the first century church used sophistry to grow their ministries by manipulating people and boasting about their success. Paul will defend himself later in 2 Corinthians with what was known as "inoffensive self-praise," an ethical response to sophistic self-promotion. Paul will boast about his weaknesses to give glory to God, not man while defending his integrity against his critics (WITH, p. 385).

Paul has renounced (ἀπειπάμεθα) the pragmatism of the super-apostles. The verb is best understood as an indirect middle indicating that true Christian leaders renounced these methods for themselves (HAN, p.319); ATR, p.810). It is a timeless Aorist tense, so Paul was not saying that they had practiced these methods in the past (RIEN, p.462). True Christian leaders disown such methods as the means to grow a church in any age.

We must renounce "the hidden things" (τὰ κρυπτὰ) "of shame" (τῆς αἰσχύνης). Paul refers to secret things or places (BAGD, p.454). The word translated "shame" (αἰσχύνης) can mean either something shameful or disgraceful (BAGD, p.25). The genitive can be used with either an objective or subjective sense. Used in the objective sense, Paul would be saying "the hidden things that bring disgrace" upon someone. Used in the subjective sense, Paul would be saying "the shame that causes honorable people to hide things." It is best to take it as a subjective genitive (MEY, p.487, fn 1). True Christian leaders renounce the things that honest people hide because they would be ashamed if others knew about those things.

What are the hidden things that embarrass honorable Christian leaders? The hidden things are the secret plans, deceptive methods, and dishonest motives that others use to accomplish their goals. Hidden things include any disguising of the truth to make it more palatable to the audience. Just because it works does not mean we should use it. The verse goes on to describe some of these hidden methods as "walking in craftiness" (πανουργία) and "adulterating or distorting (δολοῦντες) the Word of God." The word translated craftiness comes from two Greek words (πᾶν and ἔργον) which literally means "every work." The word refers to cunning pragmatism - a willingness to do whatever it takes to accomplish success (RIEN, p.462).

We must be unwilling to do whatever it takes to achieve success in the ministry. There are moral limits on our methods, even if our goals are laudable. We must renounce the use of persuasive techniques that trick and manipulate people into making professions of faith. We must avoid distorting the truth to gain a hearing with people. We must never compromise the Word of God to grow successful churches.

SHADOWY SONLIGHT

The devil does his dreadful work of blinding the minds (νοήματα) of the unbelieving. We see with our minds. The spiritual battle rages in our minds. Satan is the god of this age who blinds unbelieving minds so they cannot see the light of Christ's glory in the gospel. *And even if our gospel is veiled, it is veiled to those who are perishing, in whose case the god of this world has blinded the minds of the unbelieving so that they might not see the light of the gospel of the glory of Christ, who is the image of God* (2 Cor. 4:3-4).

Paul knew well what it meant to be blinded so that he could not see the light of the gospel despite his exceptional education and brilliant mind. The expression, "so that they might not see," is somewhat difficult to interpret. It is an infinitive attached to a preposition (εἰς τὸ μὴ αὐγάσαι). The construction is ambiguous since it can indicate either purpose or result. The Hebrew way of thinking did not distinguish sharply between purpose or result/consequence (MOU, p.142-143, fn2). Satan's purpose is to incapacitate the mind in order to keep the mind from seeing spiritual truth and his purpose, because of his power, leads to the consequence that blinded minds don't see truth.

The verb translated "see" (αὐγάσαι) has two different meanings. This verse is the only place in the New Testament, where the word is used. 1) The verb means to shine upon or illuminate an object as the sun shines upon the earth. The sense would be that Satan blinds the minds of unbelievers so that the light of the gospel does not shine upon them. 2) The verb means to see clearly or to gaze upon something or someone. In this case, Satan blinds the minds of unbelievers so that they cannot see the light of the gospel (HUGH, p.129 fn35). The latter meaning is the better one in this context. The devil incapacitates the minds of unbelievers so that they cannot gaze intently upon the light (τὸν φωτισμὸν). This meaning fits with Paul's argument in the previous chapter about the veiling that hinders people from seeing the glory (2 Cor. 3:13).

A string of genitives follows the word light. It is *the light of the gospel of the glory of Christ* (τοῦ εὐαγγελίου τῆς δόξης τοῦ Χριστοῦ). When genitives are joined together like this, the first genitive governs the following genitive so the governing genitive would be the word "gospel" (τοῦ εὐαγγελίου). Gospel is likely a genitive of origin, indicating that the light emanated from the gospel (MHT, 3:218). The next genitive, "glory" (τῆς δόξης) would describe the content of the gospel (MART, p.79). The final genitive, "of Christ" (τοῦ Χριστοῦ), would be possessive. Christ possesses the glory because He is the image (εἰκων) of God. The piling on of genitives emphasizes that Christ possesses the glory, which is the content of the gospel from which the light emanates which can save our souls. We find here a summary of Paul's argument in chapter three.

The act of witnessing engages us in spiritual warfare. We cannot pull the blinders off from the minds of unbelievers no matter how brilliant our explanations or persuasive our arguments. The devil has incapacitated their minds, and only the persuasive power of God can remove the spiritual blinding. We wonder that unbelievers don't see the glory of Christ in the gospel as we see it, but the reality is that they cannot see it because they live in a world where the Son has been eclipsed by the devil! The shadows obscure the "Sonlight" until God rips away the veil of the devil over the mind of man.

PREACHING: SAVIOR AND SELF

Self is a subtle threat to every preacher. Preaching self instead of the Savior tempts the preacher, yet no preacher can preach the Savior except through self. Truth flows through personality because every sermon is incarnational truth. The key to incarnational preaching requires self to enhance the message but not intrude upon the centrality of the Savior.

Paul wrote, *For we do not preach ourselves but Christ Jesus as Lord, and ourselves as your bond-servants for Jesus' sake* (2 Corinthians 4:5). The conjunction "and" (δὲ) is a particle used to connect two clauses where there is some contrast combined with significant continuity (BAGD, p.171). We do not preach ourselves (ἑαυτοὺς), but we do preach ourselves (ἑαυτοὺς)! We preachers must not be the message of the sermon, but we are the servants of the Savior. We must always maintain that subtle but vital distinction in our preaching.

The word translated "preach" (κηρύσσομεν) comes from the noun for "herald" (κῆρυξ) which referred to a government official commissioned to proclaim the news of the kingdom in the Greco-Roman world (NIDNTT, 3:48). The verb (κηρύσσω) is one of the most important words in the New Testament for preaching, but the New Testament writers avoided connecting the act of proclaiming truth - preaching - with the office of the Herald (NIDNTT, 3:52). Neither the office nor the person is as important as the act of proclamation to the first century preachers.

We do not proclaim ourselves "but" (ἀλλὰ) "Jesus Christ as Lord" (Ἰησοῦν Χριστὸν κύριον). Here we have a double accusative - the name and the title (RIEN, p.463). We preach the person of Jesus Christ, and the content of the Christian proclamation (κηρύγμα - kerygma) is that Christ is Lord. The content of our preaching should be the Lordship of Christ (MEY, p.491).

We preach Christ as Lord and (δὲ) ourselves (ἑαυτοὺς) as "your servants" (δούλους ὑμῶν). Once again, we have a double accusative. We do preach ourselves not as Lord but as servants of others. The incarnational content of our preaching is our servanthood. We proclaim Christ as Lord and ourselves as servants. Here is the correct balance of incarnational preaching.

The final prepositional clause "for Jesus' sake" (διὰ Ἰησοῦν) shows the motivation behind our servanthood as preachers. Some ancient manuscripts have the genitive Ἰησοῦ, which would change the meaning of the preposition διὰ to "through" (BAGD, p.179). However, the stronger evidence is for the accusative Ἰησοῦν. We are servants of those to whom we preach, but our servanthood does not negate leadership. We are not servants of people. We are servants of Jesus, and our service to people is for His sake, not their demands.

Lord, help me keep self and Savior in balance as I preach your Lordship by my servanthood.

2 CORINTHIANS 4:7-15

But we possess
7 Ἔχομεν δὲ

  this treasure in clay jars,
  τὸν θησαυρὸν τοῦτον ἐν ὀστρακίνοις σκεύεσιν,

    in order that the excess of power might be of God and not from us.
    ἵνα ἡ ὑπερβολὴ τῆς δυνάμεως ᾖ τοῦ θεοῦ καὶ μὴ ἐξ ἡμῶν·

     in every way being stressed but not distressed,
     8 ἐν παντὶ θλιβόμενοι ἀλλ' οὐ στενοχωρούμενοι,

     being confused but not despairing
     ἀπορούμενοι ἀλλ' οὐκ ἐξαπορούμενοι,

     being harassed but not abandoned,
     9 διωκόμενοι ἀλλ' οὐκ ἐγκαταλειπόμενοι,

     being knocked down but not ruined,
     καταβαλλόμενοι ἀλλ' οὐκ ἀπολλύμενοι,

    at all times carrying the death of Jesus in the body
    10 πάντοτε τὴν νέκρωσιν τοῦ Ἰησοῦ ἐν τῷ σώματι περιφέροντες,

     That the life of Jesus might be disclosed in our body
     ἵνα καὶ ἡ ζωὴ τοῦ Ἰησοῦ ἐν τῷ σώματι ἡμῶν φανερωθῇ.

For always
11 ἀεὶ γὰρ

  We who are living are being delivered to death on behalf of Jesus.
  ἡμεῖς οἱ ζῶντες εἰς θάνατον παραδιδόμεθα διὰ Ἰησοῦν,

   so that the life of Jesus might be disclosed in our mortal flesh.
   ἵνα καὶ ἡ ζωὴ τοῦ Ἰησοῦ φανερωθῇ ἐν τῇ θνητῇ σαρκὶ ἡμῶν.

   so that death operates in us but life in you.
   12 ὥστε ὁ θάνατος ἐν ἡμῖν ἐνεργεῖται, ἡ δὲ ζωὴ ἐν ὑμῖν.

But having
13 Ἔχοντες δὲ

   (having) the same spirit of faith
   (Ἔχοντες) τὸ αὐτὸ πνεῦμα τῆς πίστεως

    according to that which was written, "I believed therefore I spoke."
    κατὰ τὸ γεγραμμένον· ἐπίστευσα, διὸ ἐλάλησα,

  we also believe; therefore we also speak,
  καὶ ἡμεῖς πιστεύομεν, διὸ καὶ λαλοῦμεν,

   knowing that the one who raised the Lord Jesus
   14 εἰδότες ὅτι ὁ ἐγείρας τὸν κύριον Ἰησοῦν

   also will raise us with Jesus and will present us with you.
   καὶ ἡμᾶς σὺν Ἰησοῦ ἐγερεῖ καὶ παραστήσει σὺν ὑμῖν.

For the all (is) for your sakes,
15 τὰ γὰρ πάντα δι' ὑμᾶς,

   so that the grace which is multiplying through the many
   ἵνα ἡ χάρις πλεονάσασα διὰ τῶν πλειόνων

    might increase the thanksgiving to the glory of God.
    τὴν εὐχαριστίαν περισσεύσῃ εἰς τὴν δόξαν τοῦ θεοῦ.

PREACHING POINTS

The big idea should focus on how God uses our suffering to achieve His goals in this world. There are four major preaching points in the passage. First, God places His treasure in broken servants. Second, we see the death/life principle of Christian faith. Third, Paul talks about the relationship between our faith and our message. Fourth, our pain leads to greater glory for the Lord.

Central Idea:

1. (vs. 7-10)

2. (vs. 11-12)

3. (vs. 13-14)

4. (vs. 15)

Briefly identify two contemporary life parallels to these verses.

CLP #1

CLP #2

RARE TREASURES IN COMMON PLACES

God houses extraordinary treasures in ordinary people. It is not in the ornate palaces of the wealthy where God stores His riches. It is not the mighty and magnificent whom God uses but the humble and common people of this world. Paul wrote: *We have this treasure in earthen vessels, so that the surpassing greatness of the power will be of God and not from ourselves* (2 Cor. 4:7).

The word for "treasure" (θησαυρὸν) can mean either the place where something is kept or the treasure that is stored up (BAGD, p.361). Here Paul refers to the treasure itself and not the storeroom. The treasure could refer to the ministry because Paul started this segment with *since we have this ministry* (2 Cor. 4:1). However, the antecedent of treasure is more likely the *light of the knowledge of the glory of God in the face of Christ* because the expression is closer in context (2 Cor. 4:6). Christ's light kindled in our hearts is the treasure we have (MEY, p.494).

We hold this treasure in "clay jars" (ὀστρακίνοις σκεύεσιν). The ending on the word "clay" (ὀστρακίν-οις) indicates the material out of which something was made (RIEN, p.463). Interpreters have suggested numerous explanations for the imagery of the clay jars (MART, p.85). Paul may have been referring to small lamps which could be purchased in the stores of Corinth. The connection to the light of Christ makes this idea very possible although the Corinthian lamps, while made of clay, were often ornately decorated and fragile so not very cheap. The descriptive word "clay" more likely refers to common earthenware jars found in every home. These common clay pots were cheap and ordinary. The Jewish Rabbis taught that just as fine wine could not be stored in pots of gold but must be stored in common earthenware jars, so the wisdom of the Torah was housed in humble humans (NIDNTT, 3:914).

We find an interesting connection to storing treasure in cheap pots from the Roman triumphal processions which Paul referenced in 2 Corinthians 2:14 where he referred to us as captives in the triumphal procession exalting Christ's victory. The custom of the triumphal procession was to carry the gold and silver plunder from the victory in common earthen jars. Plutarch describes how three thousand men carried silver coins in seven hundred and fifty clay pots through the streets of Rome to celebrate a great victory over the Macedonians (HUGH, p.136).

God's greatest treasures are stored in cheap pots so that the *surpassing greatness of the power might be of God and not out of us*. The word translated "surpassing greatness" (ὑπερβολὴ) is a single word. It literally means "throwing beyond" in the sense of exceeding all boundaries, a power above all limits (HUGH, p.136, fn5). This extraordinary power (τῆς δυνάμεως) is a genitive (ablative) of source in that the surpassing greatness owes its existence in our hearts to the power of God at work in us (DM, p.82).

God's purpose (ἵνα) in housing His treasure in cheap pots like us is that the surpassing greatness of power might be (ᾖ) demonstrated to be God's and not ours. It is not "the surpassing greatness of our ministries might be of God's power." The word order argues against taking "power" with "God." It should read that "the surpassing greatness of the power might be of God and not us" (MEY, p. 495). The clause following ἵνα is an expression of "conceived result" using the present subjunctive "might be" to point to a result conceived but not yet achieved (BUR, p.92). Our ministries are not extraordinary. His power is extraordinary when housed in cheap pots like us.

Our humility in service highlights His power in ministry. We must never worry that others look down on us as ordinary because God specializes in transforming the ordinary into the extraordinary. We must also beware of elevating ourselves because the more we call attention to ourselves, the less we call attention to Him; the better we look, the worse He looks; the bigger we grow, the smaller He becomes. The more that people see us as cheap, common pots, the more His extraordinary power is visible in whatever we do for Him.

A DYING LIFE

We should not fear death because we are dying to life on earth from the moment we start life in Christ. God houses the treasure of Christ's light in the Tupperware of our lives. We are crushed and twisted by the forces of this world but never despairing or destroyed. We are *always carrying about in the body the dying of Jesus, so that the life of Jesus also may be manifested in our body* (2 Cor. 4:10).

The noun translated "dying" (νέκρωσιν) is not the word Paul normally uses for death (θάνατος, see vs. 11-12) in the New Testament (WITH, p. 387). The word (νέκρωσις) means the "process of dying or the state of being dead" (NIDNTT, 1:443). The dying of Jesus (τοῦ Ἰησοῦ) marks anyone living for Jesus. The cross is the perfect symbol for Christians because His dying shapes our living. We live dying lives.

We are carrying about (περιφέροντες) the dying of Jesus in our bodies. The verb means to carry the sick around in our arms or to carry someone we love in our hearts (BAGD, p. 653). The present tense indicates that we carry the dying of Jesus continuously throughout life. Paul places the adverb "always" (πάντοτε) first in the clause to stress the constancy of the carrying - no exceptions and no vacations!

We are constantly dying to life on earth in order to display the life of Christ in everything we do. The purpose clause (ἵνα) connects the dying to the living. The dying of Jesus (τοῦ Ἰησοῦ) parallels the life of Jesus (ἡ ζωὴ τοῦ Ἰησοῦ). God's purpose for the dying life is to reveal the life of Christ to the world. The verb translated "manifested" (φανερωθῇ) means, in the passive voice, to be revealed (BAGD, p. 852) in this case, by God. The only way for God to make known the life of Christ in us is for us to experience the death of Christ in our lives.

The death and life of Christ are displayed in our bodies, a phrase which is repeated for emphasis (ἐν τῷ σώματι). The sense is that all this dying and living takes place in our physical lives, in our bodily beings. The word "body" (σῶμα) is uniquely suited to carry this idea since it can refer either to a corpse or a living person (NIDNTT, 1:233). My bodily person is the place where I demonstrate my allegiance to his death, and the instrument God uses to display His life (MART, p. 87). Paul eliminates any possibility of Gnostic ideas separating the corporeal from the spiritual aspects of life. Christ's life is displayed in our physical lives.

The call to come to Christ is the call to die - to sacrifice my life for His life as He sacrificed His life for mine. The dying of Jesus in my personal life demonstrates the life of Jesus in my death to self. It is only as I die for Him that His life is revealed in me.

SACRIFICIAL SERVICE

Life springs from death. Like a rose blooms from earth scorched by fire, spiritual life blossoms in souls fertilized by sacrifice. Paul wrote, *For we are constantly being delivered over to death for Jesus' sake, so that the life of Jesus also may be manifested in our mortal flesh. So death works in us, but life in you* (2 Cor. 4:11-12).

The verb translated "being delivered over" (παραδιδόμεθα) frequently occurs in the passion accounts (TDNT, 2:169). It means to hand over, deliver, or give up someone. Judas handed over Jesus to the Chief Priests (Mark 14:10) and the Council handed over Jesus to Pilate (Mark 15:1). Pilate, in turn, handed over Jesus to the mob of people (Luke 23:25) by handing him over to the soldiers for crucifixion (Mark 15:15). Paul uses a passive voice to indicate that God hands over the living ones (οἱ ζῶντες) to death. The present tense of the verb tells us that this handing over to death is a constant and continual process, not a one-time event. The constancy of God delivering us to die throughout life is stressed by the opening particle "always" (ἀεὶ) placed first in the sentence for emphasis.

Serving Christ in our lives is a constant death struggle. Our death struggle has a God-ordained purpose (ἵνα καὶ). The particle translated "also" or "and" should be understood as intensive and better translated with words like "really" or "certainly." We are being delivered over to death so that the life of Jesus may really or certainly be demonstrated in our dying lives (DM, p.251). The "life of Jesus" (ἡ ζωὴ τοῦ Ἰησοῦ) is a partitive genitive meaning that the life we each have is part of all that Jesus is (MHT, *Grammar*, 3:217).

The life of a servant of Christ is a life of death. God constantly hands us over to die so that Christ's life can be revealed in our mortal flesh (θνητῇ σαρκὶ). Our flesh (σάρξ) is subject to death (θνητός). Here Paul uses the flesh in its literal sense of the material that covers our bones (BAGD, p.743). The phrase is parallel to "in the body" (ἐν τῷ σώματι) in verse 10. Our physical bodies are decaying as we live. God designs our dying process to reveal His living power, so our physical death demonstrates His spiritual life. Our willingness to die and the way we die is God's most powerful witness to the world of the power of the living Christ because the world has no answer to the dilemma of death.

Death "works" (ἐνεργεῖται) in us. We get our word energy from this Greek word. It comes from the root meaning to work and refers to action or activity. The word group was often used in the Greco-Roman world to refer to activity by cosmic or even demonic forces (TDNT, 2:652-653). In the New Testament, it is rarely used for human activity but often used of satanic miracles (2 Thess. 2:9) although even this activity functions under the authority of God (2 Thess. 2:11). The word is used elsewhere for the work of God in our lives.

Death operates in us within the parameters of God's purpose. God's purpose is to bring life to others through death operating in us. The same verb should be understood in the second half of the verse. The prepositional phrases are parallel to one another. Death works in us (ἐν ἡμῖν), but life works in you (ἐν ὑμῖν). Some think that Paul is ironic here, implying that some Christians wanted a life without hardship, unlike Paul. However, Paul is emphasizing the life of Jesus here, not life without hardship. Paul is telling them that the life of Jesus being lived in them came through Paul's willingness to die sacrificially to bring them the gospel. (HUGH, p.145).

Sacrificial love drives our missional calling. The gospel brings life to others through our willingness to die to self. Servant leadership involves nothing less than sacrificial service.

AN UNPOPULAR FAITH

Clever words can be used to produce superficially successful ministries. Modern sophists, like ancient sophists, framed their message to maximize popular appeal. They were successful. Paul was unimpressive, suffering, persecuted, and unpopular. After listing his afflictions, he writes: *But having the same spirit of faith, according to what is written, "I believed, therefore I spoke," we also believe, therefore we also speak* (2 Cor. 4:13).

The verse opens with the participle translated "having" (ἔχοντες). Although a bit awkward, it is best to take the participle as connected to the verb, "we also believe" (πιστεύομεν) later in the verse (ATR, p.1134). Everything in between the participle and the main verb is a parenthesis explaining the participle - having all this, we believe! Both the participle and the main verb are in the present tense, indicating the action of having and the action of believing are simultaneous actions (BUR, p.54). They are actions in progress.

What do we have? We have "the same spirit of faith" (τὸ αὐτὸ πνεῦμα τῆς πίστεως). The pronoun αὐτός is an attributive pronoun meaning "same" (MHT, *Grammar*, 3:194). Is Paul's spirit of faith the same as the Corinthian Christians or the psalmist he is quoting? Paul is testifying that his faith is the same as the psalmist who experienced the same struggle and victory over suffering and death (MART, p.89). The faith of the Corinthians was weak and success-oriented, while the faith of the psalmist was strong in the face of rejection.

Is the spirit the Holy Spirit or the human spirit - a big "S" or a little "s"? Grammatically it could go either way. Many take it as a small "s," referring to the human spirit or disposition of faith (HUGH, p.147). The word "faith" (πίστεως) would be taken as a subjective genitive, meaning faith stimulates the attitude or disposition we use to face adversity. It is probably better to take "Spirit" as a Big "S" referring to the Holy Spirit (MEY, p.499). Faith would be understood as an objective genitive meaning the Spirit stimulates faith in God as we face adversity. We can have confidence in God just like Paul, and his Old Testament hero had confidence because the Holy Spirit produces in us a trust in the Lord that transcends our circumstances.

Paul quotes from the Greek translation (LXX) of Psalm 116:10. The psalmist expresses praise to God for helping him through a time where he was brought low. *You have rescued my soul from death, my eyes from tears, my feet from stumbling* (Ps. 116:8). The psalmist proclaims his trust in God to see him through this trial, and then the psalmist says, *I believed there for I spoke*. Paul has this same Spirit induced faith which leads him to say - in the midst of his own sufferings - *we also believe therefore we speak*. The connective translated "therefore" (διὸ) combines the preposition διὰ with the neuter relative pronoun ὅ to form the strongest inferential connective in the New Testament (DM, p.245).

53

Speaking comes from believing. Our confession with our mouths is closely connected to the faith in our hearts (Rom. 10:9). Faith produces boldness of speech. We say what we believe even if what we say results in suffering and death. The sophists of Paul's day were mesmerizing the Corinthians with their clever words. They hid behind a politically correct style of speaking to make the message palatable to people so they could be successful just as many sophists do today. Paul is no sophist. He says what he believes although his message might be unpopular and his ministry unsuccessful in human terms (WITH, p.389).

Real faith is unpopular. Say it anyway!

OUR GLORIOUS PRESENTATION

A day is coming when we will be presented before the throne of God, perfected by His grace and completed by His power. The God who raised Jesus will raise us to stand before Him in His royal court. Paul expresses our expectation when he writes, *knowing that He who raised the Lord Jesus will raise us also with Jesus and will present us with you* (2 Corinthians 4:14). Raised with Jesus, we are presented together as His perfect re-creation, fully sanctified at last we stand as one in Christ for all eternity.

The verb translated "will present" (παραστήσει) means to present in a formal, even legal, context (BAGD, p. 627-628). For example, Jesus' parents presented the infant to the Lord in consecration at the temple in accordance with the Mosaic law following the days of purification (Luke 2:22). We, too, will be presented in consecration to the Lord at the resurrection of all believers. The predictive future can be either a simple assertion or a future promise (BUR, p.34), but here Paul asserts the fact more than he promises the future. It will happen!

God will present "us with you," Paul writes. The "us" (ἡμᾶς) is carried over from the previous clause. God will raise us (ἡμᾶς) "with Jesus" (σὺν Ἰησοῦ) and will present us "with you" (σὺν ὑμῖν), Paul tells his readers. All believers, leading apostles, and normal Christians will be presented together as one glorious church raised with Jesus to eternal glory. Paul has absolute confidence that we will all experience the consummation together. No one runs ahead of anyone in the quest for glorification, and no one stands above anyone in the presence of God Almighty.

The New Testament commonly uses the verb with a strong sense of service (TDNT, 5:840). Who do we serve? Paul uses the same word to show us that we must not present our bodies to serve sin, but we should present our bodies to serve righteousness resulting in sanctification (Rom. 6:13,19). In this life, we wrestle with that question, but there is coming a day when God will present us to perfectly serve Him forever finally freed from the presence of all sin. We will serve our King alone. The word was used to picture servants as standing in a position of honor before kings in the ancient world. We will stand before the King of Kings in His royal court as honored servants following the resurrection.

The verb can have a legal connotation meaning to stand before a judge (TDNT, 5:840). There is, perhaps, a hint of judicial review in the imagery of this verse since the context of the presentation following the resurrection leads to our standing before the Judgement Seat of Christ (2 Corinthians 5:10) where we are finally and irrevocably glorified (MEY, p.500). Christ saves us to present us

(Colossians 1:22) blameless and beyond reproach. The Judgment Seat of Christ is ultimately a purifying process - the end of our sanctification (1 Corinthians 3:10-15). All the dross is burned off and what remains is perfect. We become perfect servants to the King of Kings on that painfully glorious day.

Our goal as leaders is, like Paul, to present others to Christ perfect and pure (Colossians 1:28). We, like Paul, are jealous with a godly jealousy for those we lead to Christ because we want to present them to Christ as a father presents his pure virgin daughter to her husband (2 Corinthians 11:2). On that glorious day, the church - the bride of Christ - will be presented spotless to Christ, our groom. We will all finally be the gloriously pure bride Jesus came to save!

CHURCH GROWTH FOR GOD'S GLORY

Growing God's church God's way means dying so others can live. *Death operates in us but life in you*, Paul wrote (2 Cor. 4:12). Serving others is God's model for church growth. Sacrificial service for others produces greater glory for God. *All things are for your sakes so that the grace which is spreading to more and more people may cause the giving of thanks to abound to the glory of God* (2 Cor. 4:15).

We do all that we do as leaders on behalf of you, Paul asserts. The preposition (διά) with the accusative (ὑμᾶς) indicates the reason why something happens and can be translated "because of" or "for the sake of" someone (BAGD, p.181). Paul is saying that because of you or for your sakes we are serving - dying that you might live.

The purpose of the service is found in the clause introduced by "so that" (ἵνα). Paul serves so that grace might grow the gratitude of the believers. Grace is the subject of the clause. The main verb is "might grow" (περισσεύσει). The verb means to cause to abound or to make extremely rich (BAGD, p.651). The object of the verb is gratitude (τὴν εὐχαριστίαν). We get our English word "Eucharist" from this word. It means to give thanks or to praise someone. Our service to others causes thanksgiving to grow. Expressions of praise abound toward God because our sacrificial service exhibits His grace.

How?

The intervening clause explains how grace grows thanksgiving. Grace is described as increasing or multiplying. The nominative feminine participle modifies and explains the grace, which is nominative feminine. The word means to have more than is necessary or even to have too much (BAGD, p.667). God's grace is multiplying by means of more and more people experiencing the grace. Here the preposition (διά) is used with the genitive translated "more and more" (τῶν πλειόνων) to indicate the means or the instrument by which something happens. How does grace grow thanksgiving? Grace grows thanksgiving by multiplying the number of people who experience God's grace.

The comparative translated "more and more" (τῶν πλειόνων) combined with the double verbs for increasing stresses quantity. It is a numerical term, so "more and more people" is a good translation, but it also could mean "majority" (MOU, p.108). Paul may be alluding to the majority of the church as opposed to the minority who were against him in the conflict at Corinth. Not everybody in Corinth experienced the growing grace of God in their lives, so not everyone was abounding in thanksgiving. The same clause is used in 2 Cor. 2:6 to refer to the majority of the church that exercised church discipline. The church in Corinth was divided in conflict (WITH, p.389). God's grace increased in most of them but not all of them. The majority, however, in Corinth were so zealous for the Lord that their zeal stirred up the majority (τοὺς πλείονας) of the church in Achaia (2 Cor. 9:2) to give themselves sacrificially!

Numbers matter but only as more people, truly changed by God's grace, are motivated to give more thanks to God. Numbers matter but only as the greater numbers produce greater glory to God. We do not serve for self. We serve for Him. All of our thanksgiving abounds to the glory of God (εἰς τὴν δόξαν τοῦ θεοῦ). It all comes because of sacrifice. Dying is God's method of growing the church, so He gets the glory for the undeserved grace.

To the glory of God!
εἰς τὴν δόξαν τοῦ θεοῦ

2 CORINTHIANS 4:16-18

Therefore, we do not give up,
16 Διὸ οὐκ ἐγκακοῦμεν,

    Although our outer man is wasting away,
    ἀλλ' εἰ καὶ ὁ ἔξω ἡμῶν ἄνθρωπος διαφθείρεται,

    yet our inner man is being renewed day by day
    ἀλλ' ὁ ἔσω ἡμῶν ἀνακαινοῦται ἡμέρᾳ καὶ ἡμέρᾳ.

Because our temporary limited suffering
17 τὸ γὰρ παραυτίκα ἐλαφρὸν τῆς θλίψεως ἡμῶν

        comparing much greater with far greater
        καθ' ὑπερβολὴν εἰς ὑπερβολὴν

    an eternal weight of glory
    αἰώνιον βάρος δόξης

is achieving in us,
κατεργάζεται ἡμῖν,

    while not paying attention to what we are seeing
    18 μὴ σκοπούντων ἡμῶν τὰ βλεπόμενα

    But what (we) are not seeing
    ἀλλὰ τὰ μὴ βλεπόμενα·

        for the things we are seeing (are) transitory
        τὰ γὰρ βλεπόμενα πρόσκαιρα,

        but the things we are not seeing (are) eternal.
        τὰ δὲ μὴ βλεπόμενα αἰώνια.

PREACHING POINTS

We should frame the big idea around the truth that an eternal perspective keeps us from quitting under the pressures of temporal ministry. There are two major preaching points in the passage. The first centers around encouragement in our service for Christ. The second explains the reason and the process for persevering in ministry.

Central Idea:

1. (vs. 16)

2. (vs. 17-18)

Briefly identify two contemporary life parallels to these verses.

CLP #1

CLP #2

THE RIPTIDE OF DESPAIR

Spiritual growth is slow. People change incrementally. Ministry can feel like an exercise in futility at times. We preach our hearts out on Sunday only to face the "same old, same old" church problem on Tuesday. We pour our energy into ministry, but the church moves by centimeters to accomplish Christ's great commission. Squabbles erupt. Spiritual apathy rules. After the spiritual high on Sunday, discouragement can settle over us like a wet blanket on Monday. The same battle with discouragement happens not only for pastors but for every follower of Christ when the blows of life and the weariness of serving take their toll on our emotions.

Paul understood how easily the undertow of frustration could lead into the riptide of despair when he wrote: *Therefore, we do not lose heart, but though the outer man is decaying, yet our inner man is being renewed day by day* (2 Cor. 4:16). The word translated "lose heart" (ἐγκακοῦμεν) means to become tired or succumb to despair. It is a present indicative expressing a statement of fact that is an ongoing reality of life. Paul used the same word earlier in this section (2 Cor. 4:1) to warn us about the soul weariness of life. The word was used of women in childbirth reaching a point where they are ready to give up and fear even for life (BAGD, p.215). Despair destroys the will to live, but we are not succumbing to despair as long as we look to the Lord.

Why? The "but ... but" (ἀλλ᾽ ... ἀλλ᾽) that follows in the sentence expresses the process of fighting despair. The first "but" introduces the condition we face and the second "but" explains the confidence we have. The first "but" is followed by the words "if also" (εἰ καὶ) translated "although." The phrase expresses a condition assumed to be true (RIEN, p.465) and is concessive in force (HAN, p.320). The "but" that follows a "but if" (ἀλλ᾽ εἰ) means yet or certainly (BD, p.233). The first "but" explains the condition we feel and the second "but" introduces the solution already taking place in our lives. Despair will end one day. It will not last forever!

Our current condition is an "outer man" condition (ὁ ἔξω ἡμῶν ἄνθρωπος). The outer man is a reference to our physiological bodies (BAGD, p.279) consumed by the interplay between our feelings and our tiredness. As our energy wears down, our feelings rise up. Our outer man is constantly being destroyed (διαφθείρεται). The verb is a present tense indicating a continual process. It is passive, indicating that other forces are at work to deplete the outer man. The word was used for the dying process of animals and for abortion (MM, p.157). It can refer to rusting away, spoiling or corrupting activity (BAGD, p.190). Our outer man is constantly decaying, rusting away and wearing down because of the forces at work on us in this world.

Yet the certainty is that our inner man (ὁ ἔσω ἡμῶν) is constantly being renewed (ἀνακαινοῦται). The phrase is used in Romans 7:22 to refer to our inner nature. It is a present tense indicative verb telling us that the process is happening even in our discouraging circumstances. Paul may have coined the word himself (M&M, *Vocabulary*, p.34) because it is a compound verb formed from the preposition ἀνά meaning "in the middle" (BAGD, p.49) and καινίζω meaning "to make new" (BAGD, p.394) or the cognate adjective καινός meaning new. The reality is that our inner nature is in the middle of constantly being made new. The passive voice tells us that our inner nature is being made new by an outside force, namely God. The renewal is day by day (ἡμέρα καὶ ἡμέρα), a Hebraism meaning "every day" (BD, p.107). Our inner man has not yet arrived but is in process constantly.

How do we avoid being swept away by the riptide of despair that threatens to drown us with negativity? The undertow of discouragement is normal. We all experience it. The riptide of despair will drown us unless we stop swimming against the current and turn to the one who can rescue us from the riptide. The Lord is making us new in our inner man through the struggles of the outer man. God cares more about our inner man, and we must learn to look at what He is doing in our inner man to avoid the despair of the outer man. We are dying, but in our dying, we are being made new by His power.

THE RELATIVITY OF LIGHT AND HEAVY

Sometimes life is the pits. Pressure mounts. Circumstances compress our options to slim and none. We have two choices in the pits. We can compare our situation to our personal expectations and be discouraged. Or we can compare our circumstances to the end result of God's process and be encouraged. When we compare our plight to others in this life, our burden feels heavy. When we compare our circumstances to His eternal plan, our load is light. Light and heavy are relative to the standard we use to measure the weight. Paul wrote: *For momentary, light affliction is producing for us an eternal weight of glory far beyond all comparison* (2 Cor. 4:17).

Paul sets up a parallelism here.

momentary, light affliction
Vs.
eternal, weight of glory

Momentary (παραυτίκα) is the opposite of eternal (αἰώνιον). Light (ἐλαφρὸν) is the opposite of weight (βάρος). Affliction (θλίψεως) is the opposite of glory (δόξης). The word translated "momentary" means "on the spot" or "for the present" (BAGD, p.623). The trials we face are temporary - until life ends or the Lord returns (RIEN, p.465). The word translated "light" means easy to bear or insignificant. It can even mean frivolous or fickle! (BAGD, p.248). The word translated "affliction" means pressure generally brought on by outside circumstances (BAGD, p.362). Distress or tribulation presses us down from circumstances beyond our control.

The insignificant, frivolous pressures we find ourselves experiencing in life are producing for us an eternal and glorious result. The verb translated "producing" (κατεργάζεται) is in the present tense indicating that the action is ongoing action taking place in our lives right now. The verb means to achieve or accomplish something (BAGD, p.421). The pressures we face now are - right now - achieving something of inestimable value for us.

The value being accomplished is eternally weighty in glory. The expression "weight of glory" (βάρος δόξης) is likely a play on words from the Hebrew Scriptures. The Hebrew word for "glory" can mean either to be heavy or to be honored. Job uses the word to refer to his grief being heavier than the sands of the sea (Job 6:3), but he also says that his sons might achieve honor or glory that he does not know about (Job 14:21). The same word is used for both heavy and glory (NIC, 3:64). Since value was often determined by weight, there was a natural correspondence between weighty and glorious. Even in English, we speak of something as weighty in importance.

Our burdens are not light by themselves. Our burdens are light by comparison. The Greek text places "far beyond all comparison" (καθ᾽ ὑπερβολὴν εἰς ὑπερβολὴν) between the two corresponding descriptions to emphasize the significance of the comparison. Paul has already used this same expression earlier in his letter to the Corinthians to stress that he was "burdened excessively" (καθ᾽ ὑπερβολὴν) beyond his strength so that he despaired of life (2 Cor. 1:8)! Burdens can certainly be excessive. We can feel overwhelmed by the pressures to the point that we become discouraged. Paul does not deny that reality. Paul says that by comparison, the burdens are light because they are producing in us something much greater. Here Paul uses a double expression of excessiveness, which is difficult to translate literally. Literally, our pressures are transformative to the degree that they are beyond measure to an extraordinary extent. The glory produced is "out of all proportion" to the pressure experienced! RIEN, p.465).

As extreme pressure and high heat produce expensive diamonds, the same elements are producing great glory for us. Buried under mountains of affliction, God is creating over time His glorious masterpieces forever.

THE SLOUGH OF DESPOND AND THE SUCCESS SYNDROME

How do we measure success in ministry? If we compare our ministries to other ministries, we will evaluate our success by "nickels and noses." Buildings and budgets, attendance, and programs become tangible markers for ministry success. A comparison of these visible markers of ministry breeds either pride or despair, depending on our success or lack of success. Discouragement drags us down as we look at what we see instead of what we can't see. Paul tells us that we avoid discouragement as long as *we are not looking at the things which are seen, but* (we are looking at) *the things which are not seen because the things which are seen are temporary, but the things which are not seen are eternal* (2 Cor. 4:18).

The expression "while we are not looking at" (μὴ σκοπούντων ἡμῶν) is a genitive absolute explaining why our "light affliction" (v.17) does not cause us to lose heart (v.16). The use of the negative μὴ instead of οὐ indicates that the verb carries a conditional force (MART, p.92). We do not become discouraged in ministry provided that, or if, we are not looking at the things which are seen. Our eyes are fixed on the things which are not seen, giving us the perspective necessary to avoid discouragement.

The two verbs for "looking" are significantly different. The verb translated as long as we are not looking at (σκοπέω) carries connotations that the more general verb for looking (βλέπω), used four times in this verse, does not have. The generic "looking" (βλέπω) refers to mere sight, that which we see with our eyes. The more specific "looking" (σκοπέω) means to examine critically, to inspect carefully, like a judge examines the facts. The noun form (σκοπός) refers to a scout or watcher on the wall of a city. It can mean a target or a goal (TDNT, 7:413-416). Paul uses the noun when he says, *I press on toward the goal (σκοπός) for the prize of the upward call of God in Christ Jesus* (Phil. 3:14).

We aim our gaze at the things which are not seen to avoid discouragement because the things which are seen are temporary (πρόσκαιρα). The word is better translated temporary, not temporal (Hughes,

2 Corinthians, p.159, fn 14). The things which are seen are time-limited not merely time described. The visible things of this world, including the visible markers for ministry success, have a shelf life. The end date is stamped on all buildings and budgets. Measuring ministry by nickels and noses measures our success by that which ends instead of that which lasts forever.

What controls the focus of our lives? Where do we concentrate our sight? The church at Corinth to whom Paul was writing this letter was consumed with conflict which had discouraged him in the ministry (2 Cor. 2:12-13; 7:5-6). The false apostles who were leading the people astray were highly successful in matters that were visible. They boasted about their visible ministry success (WITH, p.390). Paul will address those boastings extensively later in his letter (2 Corinthians 10-13). Christians driven by the status and power visible in society will be consumed by disagreements about ministry. Conflict in church rises from an earthly focus. We need a whole new way of thinking about life if we are to avoid the success syndrome that leads to the slough of despond (2 Cor. 4:1, 16).

Aim determines attitude! Aiming at temporary and visible ministry success breeds discouragement. Aiming at eternal and invisible ministry goals keeps us encouraged in His service.

2 CORINTHIANS 5:1-21

2 CORINTHIANS 5:1-5

For we understand that
Οἴδαμεν γὰρ ὅτι
>If our earthly house of the tent is dismantled,
>ἐὰν ἡ ἐπίγειος ἡμῶν οἰκία τοῦ σκήνους καταλυθῇ,
>(then) we possess a building from God,
>οἰκοδομὴν ἐκ θεοῦ ἔχομεν,
>>a house that is not man-made
>>οἰκίαν ἀχειροποίητον
>>eternal in the heavens.
>>αἰώνιον ἐν τοῖς οὐρανοῖς.

For indeed
2 καὶ γὰρ
>In this home, we are groaning
>ἐν τούτῳ στενάζομεν τὸ οἰκητήριον
>>yearning to put on our home from heaven,
>>ἡμῶν τὸ ἐξ οὐρανοῦ ἐπενδύσασθαι ἐπιποθοῦντες,
>Inasmuch as
>**3** εἴ γε καὶ
>>By putting (it) on
>>ἐκδυσάμενοι
>>we will not be found naked.
>>οὐ γυμνοὶ εὑρεθησόμεθα.

For indeed
4 καὶ γὰρ
>While being in the tent, we are groaning being weighed down
>οἱ ὄντες ἐν τῷ σκήνει στενάζομεν βαρούμενοι,
>>because we do not wish
>>ἐφ’ ᾧ οὐ θέλομεν
>>>to be unclothed
>>>ἐκδύσασθαι
>>>but to be clothed,
>>>ἀλλ’ ἐπενδύσασθαι,
>>in order that what is mortal might be swallowed by the life
>>ἵνα καταποθῇ τὸ θνητὸν ὑπὸ τῆς ζωῆς.

Now the one who prepared us
5 ὁ δὲ κατεργασάμενος ἡμᾶς
>For this very thing (is) God,
>εἰς αὐτὸ τοῦτο θεός,
>>the one who gave us the down payment of the Spirit
>>ὁ δοὺς ἡμῖν τὸν ἀρραβῶνα τοῦ πνεύματος.

PREACHING POINTS

Three times Paul uses the particle "for" (γὰρ) followed by the particle "now" (δὲ) leading to four preaching points. The central idea revolves around our desire to enjoy our new bodies in eternity. Paul uses words like "groaning," "yearning," and "wish" to describe his emotional desire for a glorified body. The four preaching points give the reasons why our new bodies are important elements of our great hope in Christ.

Central Idea:

1. (vs. 1)

2. (vs. 2-3)

3. (vs. 4)

4. (vs. 5)

Briefly identify two contemporary life parallels to these verses.

CLP #1

CLP #2

COLLAPSING OUR TENTS FOR OUR UPWARD CLIMB

I used to enjoy backpacking in the mountains. We often slept in our tents. The next morning I would fold up the tent and tie it to the backpack. The rule of tent camping is to leave no trace behind as we move on to new heights. Death is like collapsing a tent. Paul writes *For we know that, if our earthly house, the tent, is taken down, we have a building from God* which is eternal (2 Corinthians 5:1).

The conditional clause (ἐὰν) is a third-class condition called a "more probable future condition" (DM, p.290). Death is a relatively uncertain future event since Christ could return before we die, but death is certainly more probable than not! Death always involves the loss of our earthly (ἐπίγειος) house (οἰκία). Paul uses the noun οἰκία instead of οἶκος, which may imply an intentional distinction. The noun οἶκος was used to refer to the totality of a deceased person's possessions while the noun οἰκία referred to simply the person's residence (TDNT, 5:131). Our physical body is the residence of our soul.

My body is a house which is a tent. The noun for a tent (σκήνους) is a genitive of apposition to the noun for a house (οἰκία). The genitive of apposition is a second noun that describes the material that makes up the first noun, so the tent is the fabric that composes the house (MHT, *Grammar*, 3:214).

Paul, as a tentmaker, knew tents. Tents were used as the cover of a wagon or a shelter on the deck of a ship along with homes used by nomadic people. They were always transitory structures in comparison to houses and even secular writers compared life in this world to a tent "passing by; one comes, sees and departs" as Democritus wrote (NIDNTT, 3:811). A Jewish reader may well have thought about The Feast of Tabernacles or Booths where families constructed tents made of branches to remember life in the wilderness before entering the promised land (RIEN, p.466).

Campers "strike" their tents every morning. The verb translated "torn down" (καλυθῇ) is a passive verb referring to the dismantling of a tent by someone other than the tenter so God "strikes" our tents in His time. It is a compound verb made up of κατά, meaning downward, and λύω, meaning to loosen. The sense of the verb is to take down the tent (TDNTT, 4:338). The bodies where our souls reside are taken down, folded up or dismantled so we can move on to new lives because our physical bodies are temporary and impermanent.

Death means collapsing the tents of our bodies for our upward climb in Christ. Our focus in death is to look forward to life not backward at life. We look ahead not behind like a backpacker eager for his next glorious mountain peak experience.

GROANING FROM LONGING

There is a groaning that rises from a deep longing for something anticipated with great excitement like a child impatiently awaits Christmas morning or a groom longs for his wedding day. Paul writes, *For even in this (house) we groan, longing to be dressed with our home from heaven* (2 Cor. 5:2).

The verb translated "we groan" (στενάζομεν, see 5:4) is a present indicative indicating that the groaning is an ongoing, continuous groaning in present time. We sigh in this life because of our circumstances (RIEN, p.466), but do our sighs reflect a negative or positive outlook? Paul says that we groan in anticipation of something better not merely distress over our bad circumstances. Our groaning reflects a positive outlook for the future and is generated by the Holy Spirit at work in our lives according to Romans 8:23, where Paul uses the same word (MART, p.104). Groaning is *the first fruits of the Spirit* as we await *the redemption of our body*. Sighing for heaven is the sign of the Spirit in our hearts.

We groan because we long to be dressed in our home from heaven. The verb translated "longing" (ἐπιποθοῦντες) is a present participle indicating that we are continually longing to be clothed. We long for our heavenly clothing like newborn babies long for pure milk (1 Peter 2:2). Paul tells us that we will all be changed - transformed - at the resurrection as the perishable puts on the imperishable and the mortal puts on immortality (1 Cor. 15:51-53). The believer's longing is to put on the imperishable body that will last forever.

Paul uses the metaphor of a house (οἰκητήριον), but he changes the word from οἰκία to οἰκητήριον. The latter word implies a home more than a house (HUGH, p.168, fn 29). A house (οἰκία) does not require an inhabitant to be a house. A home (οἰκητήριον) implies the presence of an inhabitant (οἰκητήρ). Paul's mixed metaphor enriches our understanding. We long for the day when we will be dressed in a home from heaven. We will inhabit our heavenly bodies as our eternal homes.

The verb translated "to be clothed or dressed" (ἐπενδύσασθαι) is a compound word combining the preposition ἐπί with the verb ἐνδύω. The meaning of the compound verb is to put on outer clothes over other clothes like an overcoat is put on over regular clothing. Our heavenly body is put on over our earthly body in a way that absorbs and transforms our earthly body (HUGH, p.168 fn31). Since we get our glorified bodies to wear at the resurrection when Christ returns and not when we die, we long to be alive until the return of Christ and experience the glorious transformation without death (1 Cor. 15:51-53).

We do not fear death but long to avoid the disembodied state Paul calls "nakedness" in the next verse (2 Cor. 5:3). Death brings nakedness until God dresses us with our new bodies at the resurrection. It is far better to be alive when Christ returns because God puts on our new bodies like an overcoat covering and transforming our current bodies.

We sigh with longing for that day. I watched my dad in his last year of life groaning with a deep desire to be clothed with his heavenly home. He suffered physically, but he sighed not so much because of his physical suffering but because of his desire for heaven. His groaning rose from his longing. Earth holds little value when the longings of our heart transfuse our horizon with the glorious hues of heaven.

WILL WE HAVE BODIES IN HEAVEN?

Physical death is the separation of the soul from the body. We know two important truths about death and the afterlife. 1) To be absent from our bodies is to be present with our Lord (2 Cor. 5:8). 2) We receive our new bodies at the resurrection when Christ returns (1 Cor. 15:50-54). What happens to us in the interim, between death and the resurrection? We go to heaven, but will we have bodies in heaven?

Paul gives us a clue in 2 Corinthians 5:1-4. When the tent that is our body is folded up in death, we know we have an eternal home to clothe our souls, yet Paul expresses a longing to be clothed at death. Why? So as not to be seen as naked. Paul writes in verse three, "*of course if* (εἴ γε καὶ, see HUGH, p.169, fn32) *having clothed ourselves* (ἐνδυσάμενοι), *we will not be discovered* (εὑρεθησόμεθα) *naked* (γυμνοὶ)." Textual note: the reading "having put on" (ἐνδυσάμενοι) is better attested than the reading "having put off" (ἐκδυσάμενοι) even though it might seem tautological (METZ, p.579-580).

What does Paul mean by expressing his desire not to be found naked? There are three popular options. 1) Paul is talking about his desire not to experience the suffering and shame of our current mortal lives any longer (BKC, 2 Cor. 5:3). 2) Paul is talking about his desire for a temporary intermediate body that God gives to us until the resurrection (WOY, p.98-103). 3) Paul is talking about his fervent wish not to be found in a bodiless state after death until the coming of Christ (HUGH, pp.169-173).

The third interpretation is best. Paul is expressing a concern he feels about what happens after death and his desire to be clothed rather than unclothed after he dies (2 Cor. 5:4). The future tense "will be found naked" (εὑρεθησόμεθα) is a future fear, not a present reality. The experience of "nakedness" follows death. Why express his concern at all if he knows already he will be clothed immediately with his new body when he dies? Furthermore, the intermediate body is nowhere else taught in Scripture and seems foreign to New Testament theology (HUGH, p.173).

Paul wants to be alive until Christ returns so he can skip the disembodied intermediate state between death and the resurrection (MART, p.106). Paul does not fear death, and neither should we, but he does not want death either. He is like the martyrs under the throne of heaven crying "How long, O Lord" (Rev. 6:9-10). These disembodied souls were waiting in heaven for the coming of Christ to judge the world.

I draw four conclusions from Paul's longing not to be discovered naked after death.

1) God created humans to be complete as soul and body together. Our souls were never designed to live bodiless like the Platonic (and later Gnostic) idea that our souls have been imprisoned by our bodies and long to be freed from bodily existence. We are less than fully human without a body, so our bodies are vital to the fullness of eternal life (HUGH, p.170).

2) We live as disembodied souls in heaven between death now and the resurrection to come. Yet, somehow, in a way we find hard to grasp, our souls will still be recognizable to others during this interim period.

3) It is far, far better to remain alive until the coming of Christ and so enter immediately into the fullness of resurrected life. Our "blessed hope" (Titus 2:13) is to see Jesus at His appearing and never experience death at all.

4) We know for certain that to die is gain (Phil 1:21) - even in our disembodied state. We prefer to be separated from our bodies because we are, then, at home with our Lord (2 Cor. 5:8).

Even so, Lord, come quickly!

SWALLOWED BY LIFE

Christians do not look forward to death. We look forward to life. Death is plan "B" for the Christian, not plan "A." Plan "A" is to be alive when Christ returns so we can be transformed directly into our resurrection bodies without the stripping that we experience in death. Death strips the body from the soul, leaving us naked until the coming of Christ when we receive our resurrection bodies. Paul writes, *while we are in this tent, we groan, being burdened, because we do not want to be unclothed but to be clothed, so that what is mortal will be swallowed up by life* (2 Cor. 5:4).

We are groaning in these earthly bodies as people who are weighed down (βαρούμενοι) by a depressing thought (RIEN, p.466). We know that death is coming for all of us unless Jesus comes back first. What we will experience in death is the cause of our mental burden. The next clause begins with a causal connection (ἐφ' ᾧ) explaining the reason for the depressing weight we carry in life (MHT, 3:272). We want to be clothed (ἐπενδύσασθαι) with a new body not stripped (ἐκδύσασθαι) of the old body and left naked until the resurrection (2 Cor. 5:3). We don't want to die and live in a bodiless state. God never designed the soul to be separate from the body as Greek philosophy, and later Gnosticism promoted. God created the soul and body as one whole being in perfect unity. Sin brought the curse of death which is the separation of the soul from the body.

We want to be clothed so that the mortal will be swallowed up by the life. Mortal (θνητὸν) means that which is subject to death (BAGD, p.362). Our bodies, not our souls, are subject to physical death. Paul uses the euphemism of a "tent" (σκήνει) to describe our bodies because a tent is a temporary form of housing. Our bodies will be swallowed up by life at the resurrection. The verb translated "swallowed up" (καταποθῇ) is a picturesque term. The compound verb comes from the preposition κατά meaning "down" and the verb πίνω meaning "to drink." The compound verb means to "drink down" or "swallow" (BAGD, p.416).

The word was also used of waves of water overwhelming someone. The Septuagint uses the word to describe how God drowned the Egyptians in the Red Sea (Exodus 15:4). Life drinks down that which is subject to death. Our mortal bodies are absorbed into life when Christ comes back (HUGH, p.170). The same verb is used by Paul in 1 Corinthians 15:54 when he writes that "death is drowned (swallowed up) in victory."

Our mortal bodies are swallowed by the life. The preposition (ὑπὸ) with a genitive object and a passive verb as in this case denotes the agent that does the swallowing, not the instrument by which we are swallowed (BD, p.122). The swallower of death is the life (τῆς ζωῆς). Normally the definite article is not used with abstract nouns like "life" (BD, p.134) so the question is, why is the article used in this case? The definite article is used with nouns designating persons (BD, p.133) so "the life" is a substitute for a person, not an abstract noun. Jesus is "the life" (John 14:6) so Jesus, as the life, swallows up our mortal bodies when He returns for us (HUGH, p.170, fn35).

We want to be alive when Christ comes back so we can be drowned by life in Him. When Christ comes back, He immerses us in the tsunami of His life. Jesus, who is life itself, swallows us, who are subject to death, alive, so we never taste the curse of death.

2 CORINTHIANS 5:6-10

Being confident
6 Θαρροῦντες

therefore
οὖν

      always
      πάντοτε
and understanding that
καὶ εἰδότες ὅτι
      while being at home in the body
      ἐνδημοῦντες ἐν τῷ σώματι
      we are away from home
      ἐκδημοῦμεν
         separated from the Lord
         ἀπὸ τοῦ κυρίου·
            for by means of faith we are living, not by means of sight
            7 διὰ πίστεως γὰρ περιπατοῦμεν, οὐ διὰ εἴδους·

we are confident indeed
8 θαρροῦμεν δὲ
And we want rather
καὶ εὐδοκοῦμεν μᾶλλον
      to be away from home out of the body
      ἐκδημῆσαι ἐκ τοῦ σώματος
      and to live at home with the Lord.
      καὶ ἐνδημῆσαι πρὸς τὸν κύριον.

Wherefore also
9 διὸ καὶ
    We aspire
    φιλοτιμούμεθα,
        whether at home or away from home
        εἴτε ἐνδημοῦντες εἴτε ἐκδημοῦντες,
    to be pleasing to Him.
    εὐάρεστοι αὐτῷ εἶναι.
For it is necessary that we all be exposed
10 τοὺς γὰρ πάντας ἡμᾶς φανερωθῆναι δεῖ
    Before the judge's seat of Christ,
    ἔμπροσθεν τοῦ βήματος τοῦ Χριστοῦ,
        in order that each one be repaid for
        ἵνα κομίσηται ἕκαστος
           the things by means of the body
           τὰ διὰ τοῦ σώματος
              in accordance with what things he has done,
              πρὸς ἃ ἔπραξεν,
                whether beneficial or evil.
                εἴτε ἀγαθὸν εἴτε φαῦλον.

PREACHING POINTS

There are two preaching points in this passage corresponding to "therefore" (οὖν) and "wherefore" (διό). The first preaching point explains our confidence that we will be at home with the Lord. The second preaching point explains our ambition both in this life and the next. We must combine the concepts of confidence and ambition into one big idea.

Central Idea:

1. (vs. 6-8)

2. (vs. 9-10)

Briefly identify two contemporary life parallels to these verses.

CLP #1

CLP #2

LIVING AS IMMIGRANTS

Living in our physical bodies is like living in a foreign country far from home. We think we are at home in these bodies, but we long for our eternal, heavenly bodies whenever we suffer demoralizing pain and sickness. We instinctively know as Christians we were made for heaven and expect that God will transport us there one day, reconfiguring our bodies into forms fit for the new world. Being always confident (2 Cor. 5:6), we are confident (2 Cor. 5:8) that one day we will be at home with Jesus. The participle "being confident" (θαρροῦντες) introduces a break in the sentence, and the thought is picked up again in verse 8 with the main verb "we are confident" (θαρροῦμεν).

The intervening thought is introduced by "and knowing that" (καὶ εἰδότες ὅτι). The conjunction (καὶ) should not be understood as causal - because we know a truth. Paul introduces an additional thought as a parenthesis. The additional thought is not the cause of our confidence. It explains our current status in life more fully. Our confidence is not based on our current status in life. We are always (πάντοτε) confident, no matter our circumstances. The additional thought explains our circumstances.

"While we are home in the body, we are absent from the Lord" (2 Cor. 5:6). The play on words is clearer and more vivid in the Greek text. We "are at home" translates ἐνδημοῦντες and "are absent" translates ἐκδημοῦμεν. The second word means to leave one's country or to be away from home in a foreign land (BAGD, p.238). The temporal participle, "while we are at home in the body," explains our current circumstances. We live in these bodies but living in our bodies means that we are far away from home with the Lord. We are immigrants in this life. Our true home is with Jesus.

Paul goes on to explain how we can have communion with Jesus even though we are immigrants in a foreign land. We are far away from Jesus in one sense, but we still know His presence in another because (γὰρ) "by faith we are walking, not by sight" (2 Cor. 5:7). We are walking (περιπατοῦμεν) is a present tense verb indicating the current, ongoing life we live. "By faith (διὰ πίστεως) and "by sight" (διὰ εἴδους) are on opposite ends of the sentence for contrasting emphasis. The preposition (διὰ) with the genitive indicates "by means of" (MOU, p.56). Faith and sight are opposite ways of living as immigrants in a strange land.

The noun translated "sight" has both an active and a passive meaning. The passive meaning refers to form or outward appearance. The active meaning is seeing or sight (BAGD, p.221). Some understand the verse using a passive meaning. We are not walking by what is seen (Hughes, *2 Corinthians*, p.176) in this life but by faith in Him. Living by the way things appear to be is not living by faith. Others argue for an active sense of the word. We are not walking by what we can see because we cannot see Jesus. We are living in a foreign land, and He is invisible to us. We walk by faith that He is with us even though we cannot see Him now (MART, p.111). The active sense is probably better because it forms a more vivid contrast to walking by faith.

We live in our bodies like an immigrant who has left his loved one in a foreign country. The immigrant cannot see the one he loves, but he works hard to see her again one day. We cannot see Jesus, but we work hard for the day when we shall see Him again. Believing not seeing is the only way to live in our declining and decaying bodies.

PERSONAL AMBITION

I saw a cartoon recently that pictured three fish bowls in a line, each one bigger than the previous one. The first bowl contained numerous goldfish. One goldfish jumped from the first bowl into the bigger second and then into the third and largest bowl. The caption read, "When your ambition is big, then your efforts should be even bigger." If you form a word cluster around the word "ambition," you will see words like drive, determination, aspiration, zeal, desire, goal, purpose, dream, and success. Ambition drives success in our world. We thrive on ambition.

Why then does ambition get a bad reputation among Christians? Why do we think it unspiritual to have ambitions? One reason, of course, is that worldly ambition is selfish. We cannot thrive spiritually if we are driven by selfish ambition. Godly ambition, however, is necessary for personal success as a Christian. Without ambition, we accomplish nothing for Christ. Spiritual ambition drives our desires and guides our determination in life. Paul writes; *Therefore, we also have as our ambition, whether at home or absent, to be pleasing to Him* (2 Cor. 5:9).

Paul begins with the connective "therefore" (διὸ). He is summarizing a logical conclusion which can be translated "and so" (MOU, p.164). And so we aspire (φιλοτιμούμεθα) to please Him. The verb is a compound word meaning to love (φίλος) honor (τιμάω) which is close to how we use ambitious today. It can mean to devote ourselves zealously to a cause (HUGH, p.178, fn. 54). It is a progressive present tense deponent verb indicating that we do the action continuously.

Our aspiration is true whether we are "at home" (ἐνδημοῦντες) or "absent" (ἐκδημοῦντες). We have seen these two words before in this passage (vs.6, 8). What does it mean to be at home or to be absent? Some understand it to mean whether we are at home in the body (alive on earth) or we absent from the body (naked in the intermediate state) we are to aspire to please Jesus (HUGH, 178-179). Does this mean that we must strive in our bodiless, intermediate state after death to please Christ? Obviously, this cannot be true as Hughes quickly explains. The next verse (v.10) states that we are judged only for what we do "in the body" (σώματος).

It is better to read the phrases contextually. Whether we are at home with the Lord (v.8) or absent from the Lord (v.6), our one ambition is to please Him. If we are home with the Lord, we cannot do otherwise. We will please Him because there is no way to displease Him when we are at home with Him (MART, p.113). For now, we are absent from the Lord (v.6), so our one desire is to please Him now as we await His return.

The purpose of our ambition is to be pleasing to Him. The verb "to be" (εἶναι) is a purpose infinitive (Burton, *Moods and Tenses*, p.146). The verb means to exist or to live (BAGD, p.223). "Pleasing" (εὐάρεστοι) means to be acceptable, particularly to God (Romans 12:2). Paul uses it in Titus 2:9 of slaves giving satisfaction to their masters (BAGD, p.318). Our personal ambition both now and for eternity is to bring satisfaction to Christ. We live to please Him.

An ambition to please Christ means:

- a zeal to accomplish His mission in this world
- a drive to use our gifts for His church

- a passion to invest our energy for His purpose
- a determination to be successful in His ministry

How ambitious are you? How ambitious am I?

THE GREAT REVEAL

We are quick to blame and quick to take credit. We are at the same time critical of others and defensive before our critics. We forget that there is coming a day when God will expose everything done or thought by Christians. All will be laid bare, the blame and the credit. Even our inner motives will be revealed on that day. Paul wrote, *"We must all appear before the judgment seat of Christ"* (2 Corinthians 5:10).

"We must" translates the verb "it is necessary" (δεῖ). The verb denotes compulsion of any kind but particularly emphasizes a sense of divine destiny (BAGD, p.172). We are destined to appear before the judgment seat of Christ. There are no exceptions. It is necessary for all of us (τοὺς πάντας ἡμᾶς) to face Christ's evaluation. The grammatical construction treats individuals as part of the whole (BD, p.144). Each Christian faces judgment as part of the whole church being judged.

The verb translated "appear" (φανερωθῆναι) is a passive infinitive related to the word for shining light (φαίνω) which can be translated "to appear" in the passive voice (TDNTT, 3:320, BAGD, p.851). John calls us to abide in Christ so that "when He appears" (φανερωθῇ), we will have the confidence to face Him (1 John 2:28). However, φανερόω, as opposed to φαίνω, means to reveal or show someone or something more than simply appear (BAGD, p. 852-853). A few verses earlier, John used the word to describe unbelievers who had been part of the church but who left the church. John says that by leaving the church *"it would be shown (revealed) that they all are not of us"* (1 John 2:19). Unbelievers show their true colors when they leave the church.

Paul uses the passive voice in 2 Corinthians 5:10. We are destined to be revealed by God before the judgment seat of Christ (RIEN, p.467). Paul uses φανερόω nine times in 2 Corinthians and three times in 2 Corinthians 5:10-11. He uses the passive voice all three times teaching us that God does the revealing before the judgment seat of Christ. Paul later expresses that his intention in writing to the Corinthians so harshly was to seek for God to reveal to them their own zeal for Paul (2 Cor. 7:12). Sometimes God reveals us to ourselves. We don't merely appear before the judgment seat, but God shows us to be who we are at the judgment seat (TDNTT, 3:322).

We will be stripped naked before Christ at His judgment. All our hidden sins, our hypocrisies of thought and action that we conceal so well from others will be laid bare before us as we stand before the Lord. His eyes will penetrate to our deepest secrets and rip away the respectable masks we so carefully construct for ourselves in this life. We will see ourselves for who we are both the good and the bad. God will expose both the "hypocritical and the hypercritical" on that day of His refining fire (HUGH, p.180).

"Therefore, do not go on passing judgment before the time, but wait until the Lord comes who will both bring to light (φωτίσει) the things hidden in the darkness and disclose (φανερώσει) the motives of men's hearts; and then each man's praise will come to him from God" (1 Corinthians 4:5).

Don't be quick to blame or take credit. Wait for the great reveal!

ON TRIAL

Christ's courtroom can be a scary place for Christians. We are safe by the blood of Christ but culpable for our personal actions. Our lives are an open book before His eyes. We will be judged for what we do with what He gives. Paul wrote: *For we must all appear before the judgment seat of Christ, so that each one may be recompensed for his deeds in the body, according to what he has done, whether good or bad* (2 Corinthians 5:10).

We will stand before the dais of justice someday. The word translated "judgment seat" (βήματος) referred to a raised platform where civil authorities sat to hear legal cases (NIDNTT, 2:369). The purpose (ἵνα) of Christ's tribunal for Christians is not to determine entry into heaven but to evaluate our lives on earth. Each one of us individually (ἕκαστος) will be recompensed (κομίσηται) for what we have done. The verb in the middle voice means to "get back" or "recover." In Jesus' parable of the talents, the master wanted to get back what was his with interest (Mt. 25:27). Abraham received his son back after offering him to God (Heb. 11:19). We will get back from Christ what we spend in life (BAGD, p.443).

We will get back the things (τὰ) according to what (πρὸς ἃ) we did. The preposition "according to" (πρὸς) is used in a comparative sense meaning in proportion to our deeds (Moule, *Idiom Book*, p.53). The word translated "deeds" (ἔπραξεν) is a verb, not a noun. It means to accomplish or do something. The word is never used of divine action in the New Testament and primarily emphasizes negative or neutral human activity (NIDNTT, 3:1157). Paul uses it with a neutral sense in this context since he goes on to say, "whether good or bad."

Paul is very clear that he is talking about the things we do "in the body." The prepositional clause is bracketed by the article τὰ and the relative pronoun "what" (ἃ) indicating that our reward is for our bodily actions. The prepositional clause (διὰ τοῦ σώματος) expresses the means or the instrument by which something is done. The preposition (διὰ) identifies the agent that comes between the actor and the result of the action (ATR, p.582). What we do, we do by means of the body. We are judged by what we accomplish through our bodies as the instruments of our intentions.

The Christian life is all about investment. We use our bodies to make eternal investments. Some investments are good, but some are bad. We will present to Jesus our investment portfolio when we stand before His dais of justice. Our portfolio will contain good investments and wasted opportunities, and Jesus will evaluate it all on that day. The return we receive is proportional to the amount we invested that has eternal value.

We get back in heaven what we put in on earth!

2 CORINTHIANS 5:11-15

Understanding
11 Εἰδότες

Therefore
οὖν

    the awe of the Lord
    τὸν φόβον τοῦ κυρίου

  men we are persuading,
  ἀνθρώπους πείθομεν,

  but to God we have been exposed
  θεῷ δὲ πεφανερώμεθα·

    and I hope also in your consciences we are disclosed
    ἐλπίζω δὲ καὶ ἐν ταῖς συνειδήσεσιν ὑμῶν πεφανερῶσθαι.

We are not again recommending ourselves to you
12 οὐ πάλιν ἑαυτοὺς συνιστάνομεν ὑμῖν

  But giving to you an opportunity of boasting on behalf of us,
  ἀλλὰ ἀφορμὴν διδόντες ὑμῖν καυχήματος ὑπὲρ ἡμῶν,

    in order that you have (an opportunity)
    ἵνα ἔχητε

      in the sight of the ones who boast in appearance
      πρὸς τοὺς ἐν προσώπῳ καυχωμένους

        and not in heart
        καὶ μὴ ἐν καρδίᾳ.

  For if we are insane, (it is) for God
  13 εἴτε γὰρ ἐξέστημεν, θεῷ·

    Or if we are sane, (it is) for you.
    εἴτε σωφρονοῦμεν, ὑμῖν.

For the love of Christ compresses us,
14 ἡ γὰρ ἀγάπη τοῦ Χριστοῦ συνέχει ἡμᾶς,

  concluding this
  κρίναντας τοῦτο,

    that one died on behalf of all,
    ὅτι εἷς ὑπὲρ πάντων ἀπέθανεν,

      as a result all died.
      ἄρα οἱ πάντες ἀπέθανον·

    and He died on behalf of all,
    15 καὶ ὑπὲρ πάντων ἀπέθανεν,

      in order that the living ones might no longer live for themselves
      ἵνα οἱ ζῶντες μηκέτι ἑαυτοῖς ζῶσιν

      but on behalf of Him who died and was raised to life.
      ἀλλὰ τῷ ὑπὲρ αὐτῶν ἀποθανόντι καὶ ἐγερθέντι.

PREACHING POINTS

If our ambition is to please God, as Paul has said in verse 9, then what motivates us to pursue that ambition? There are three preaching points in the passage. Each one explains a motive for pleasing God. The big idea revolves around what drives us to live totally for Christ.

Central Idea:

1. (vs. 11)

2. (vs. 12-13)

3. (vs. 14-15)

Briefly identify two contemporary life parallels to these verses.

CLP #1

CLP #2

PERSUASIVE FEAR

Fear is highly persuasive as long as we can see an effective solution. Fear boomerangs when fright outweighs the credibility of the solution. Healthy fear sees God as the holy solution. The *"fear of the Lord is the beginning of wisdom,"* the psalmist wrote (Psalm 111:10, cf. Prov. 1:7). Paul, too, knew the fear that moves our minds to know God and our wills to serve Him. *"Therefore, knowing the fear of the Lord, we persuade men, but we are revealed to God"* (2 Corinthians 5:11).

"Therefore" (οὖν) points us back to verse 10 where Paul spoke of standing before the Judgment Seat of Christ to give an account of his life. We will stand exposed, stripped naked, before the eyes of Jesus on that day. Our thoughts, actions, and motives will be revealed to us by the one who loves us more than anyone. We will know and be known. The fear of His piercing vision drives us to serve Him. The fear (τὸν φόβον) is not the terror of damnation but the reverence of love (BAGD, p.864). We will not go to hell because of His grace, but we will face His judgment because of His holiness. We fear the Lord (τοῦ κυρίου). This is an objective genitive (ATR, p.500). The person of Christ is the focus of our fear.

"Knowing" (Εἰδότες) the fear of facing Jesus we persuade men. The perfect participle is used of completed action that results in a state of existence contemporaneous with the time of the main verb (BUR, p.71). The main verb, to persuade (πείθομεν), is in the present tense, so the state of our knowing is now. We know the fear of the Lord because we have been made known to God. The perfect passive verb (πεφανερώμεθα) means to be revealed or made visible (BAGD, p.852). Already exposed before God, we know the fear of final exposure which drives us to persuade others.

The verb translated "persuade" means to convince or appeal to others (BAGD, p.639). It is a conative present. The persuasion is incomplete. A conative present emphasizes the attempt while leaving the result unknown (MHT, 3:63). Living with the knowledge that God will judge us for how we invest our lives, we try to persuade men. We make every attempt to appeal to people. We constantly seek to convince people.

What do we try to persuade others about? What is the objective of our persuasion? Paul leaves the objective unspoken. There are at least a half-dozen options that interpreters have proposed over the years (MEY, p.523). Perhaps the most popular interpretation is evangelistic. We are trying to persuade others to become followers of Christ - to become Christians. However, the context is not evangelistic, making an evangelistic emphasis suspect. The better understanding is to see the persuasion in terms of Paul's own motivation expressed in verse 9 (MEY, p.524). Our ambition is to please God, a form of fear, so we seek to persuade others to fear God, and so to please Him.

Motivated by the fear of the Lord, we persuade others to fear the Lord.

PREACHING: STYLE OR SUBSTANCE

Sophistry was popular in Paul's day, and, in Corinth, it had infiltrated the church. Preachers focused on manipulating people through style without substance, superficiality, and self-promotion. Persuasion was the purpose of rhetoric, and these oratorically skilled preachers were highly successful persuaders. They ridiculed Paul because he did not employ the techniques and styles that were successful in the world. Paul, too, sought to persuade people (2 Corinthians 5:11) but he did not utilize the showy skills of the sophists. He tried to persuade people in the fear of the Lord. Paul used rhetoric carefully and ethically.

We are not again commending ourselves to you but are giving you an occasion to be proud of us, so that you will have an answer for those who take pride in appearance and not in heart (2 Corinthians 5:12).

The sophists of Paul's day practiced four kinds of rhetoric. Epideictic rhetoric honored rulers with flowery words. Deliberative rhetoric used arguments to persuade people in a public assembly. Forensic rhetoric defended people in court settings. Declamation or ornamental rhetoric emphasized form over substance, eloquence over content (WITH, p.392). Paul used mostly deliberative rhetoric - the language of the assembly. He rejected the showiness of sophistic rhetoric commonly used by the preachers traveling through Corinth.

Paul says *we are not commending ourselves to you* even though he is obviously commending himself to them. He is rejecting the kind of commendation that the sophists used. The word "commending" (συνιστάνομεν) means to present or recommend someone to someone (BAGD, p.790). There is some evidence to suggest that when Paul wants to disapprove of self-commendation, he places the pronoun before the verb as in this case (ἑαυτοὺς συνιστάνομεν cf. 2 Corinthians 10:12). When Paul wants to approve of self-commendation, he places the pronoun after the verb (συνίσταντες ἑαυτοὺς, cf. 2 Corinthians 6:4). Paul seems to make a distinction between good and bad self-commendation in this way (WITH, p.393, fn.5).

Paul's goal in good self-commendation is to give the Christians an "occasion" (ἀφορμὴν) or opportunity for "boasting" (καυχήματος) about him. He would use rhetoric so that others could speak positively about his ministry because such "boasting" was boasting in the Lord, not in Paul. He qualifies the boasting as a way to answer those who boast in appearance, not in heart. The sophistic preachers put their faith in the latest methods and approaches to attracting people, but Paul was more interested in using rhetoric to get to the heart - the content - of the truth.

We don't want to embarrass Christians by how we look, talk, and act, so we preach in culturally appropriate styles. Whether we preach in jeans and a t-shirt or a three-piece suit is a matter of style, not substance. We use the style that fits the cultural context to give people a reason to be positive about our message. However, these are all matters of appearance (προσώπῳ), literally the "face" of the matter (BAGD, p.720). Styles are external. By themselves, they are all show but no substance. Styles and methods are not "heart" (καρδία) issues. Matters of the heart are matters of substance. We must not compromise content to achieve persuasion. Such persuasion is manipulative and deceitful. Emphasizing style over substance to reach people may be popular but leads to a superficial faith.

83

MOTIVE FOR MINISTRY

Love moves us to serve Jesus. Paul wrote, *"For the love of Christ controls us, having concluded this, that one died for all, therefore all died"* (2 Corinthians 5:14). Is it our love for Christ that motivates our ministry or Christ's love for us? His love or our love that is the question.

The expression "love of Christ" (ἀγάπη τοῦ Χριστοῦ) can be either a subjective or an objective genitive. The use of the genitive (Χριστοῦ) can only be determined by context (ATR, p.499). The phrase could be understood as an objective genitive, meaning Christ is the object of our love. However, the better interpretation is a subjective genitive meaning that Christ is the subject of the love. Christ's love for us is the basis of our love for Christ (MART, p.128).

God establishes the relationship. He initiates the love. Our love is a response to His love. Paul explains the statement by pointing to Christ's love on the cross, which is why we should take it as a subjective genitive. Paul is talking about Christ's love for us "having concluded" (κρίναντες) that He died for us. The cross is on Paul's s mind. Christ's love is the motive for his ministry. Christ's love is faithful. Our love is fickle. If our love for Christ motivates our ministry, our ministry will be like riding a roller coaster. Our love for Christ has highs and lows. Our love is inconsistent. The only solid foundation for our ministry is Christ's love for us proven on the cross. Because He loved us enough to die for us, we are moved to love Him enough to live for Him.

Christ's love "controls" us. There are three basic meanings of the word συνέχει, 1) to hold together, 2) to enclose or lock up, and 3) to oppress or overpower. The third meaning derives from the second. To enclose or hem in leads to controlling or ruling (TDNT, 7:877-879). The New Testament does not use the word to mean hold together. Luke commonly uses the word with the sense of to enclose or to close. Paul seems to use the word to mean dominate or overpower (TDNT, 7:882-883). Christ's love controls us not so much in the sense of urging us to serve but in the sense of hemming us in on all sides or pressing us into service. He locks us up in love. Christ's love confines us, limiting our choices. It may even be said that Christ's love harasses us so that we have no rest until we do all we can for Him (MEY, 6:528).

The love of Christ controls us like a narrow pipe restricts the flow of water. The velocity of the water increases as the flow of water is restricted. The intensity of our ministry increases as His love for us constricts our service for Him. We are squeezed by His love on the cross until we can do nothing else but serve Him in response. The verb (συνέχει) is a present tense indicative. Christ's love for us dominates us continually in life.

Oppressed by His love, we are pressed into His service.

LIFE'S PURPOSE

The death of Christ generates our purpose in life.

Paul wrote, *He died for all, so that they who live might no longer live for themselves, but for Him who died and rose again for them* (2 Corinthians 5:15).

He died for all repeats what Paul said in verse 14 to expand the idea of Christ's substitutionary death to our purpose for life in verse 15. Some have argued that the preposition ὑπὲρ cannot be equated with the preposition ἀντί (MEY, p.530). The latter means "instead of" while the former means "on behalf of" so here Jesus died on our behalf and not in our place according to some. The idea that the preposition ὑπὲρ can never carry a substitutionary sense is erroneous (HUGH, p.193, fn.24). The context determines the usage of the preposition, and here the context makes the preposition substitutionary. Paul says, *One died for all, so then all died* (v.14). Christ's love for us motivates us by His death in our place. The "all is the "us!"

The atonement is effective only for those who are regenerated to new life. They who died are they who live. All who died Christ's death, live Christ's life. Jesus died so that (ἵνα) the living ones (οἱ ζῶντες) might no longer live (ζῶσιν) for themselves. The present tense subjunctive verb is used to express continuing purpose (RIEN, p.469). Believers (the living ones) no longer live for themselves (ἑαυτοῖς). The pronoun is a dative of advantage. We no longer live for the advantage or benefit of ourselves once we have died to live again. We died to life for our benefit and live now for His benefit.

Regenerated people live for the one who died and rose again (τῷ ἀποθανόντι καὶ ἐγερθέντι) for them (ὑπὲρ αὐτῶν). It is possible that the prepositional phrase "for them" (ὑπὲρ αὐτῶν) should only be connected to the dying (ἀποθανόντι) and not the rising (ἐγερθέντι) because of word order. However, it is best to take both Christ's death and resurrection for us (HUGH, p.196, fn.33). The article (τῷ) governs both participles. He died our death and rose again for our life. Our sanctification is built on a substitutionary foundation just as much as our justification.

The "one who died and rose again for us" is also a dative of advantage. The two datives are parallel in the structure. Regenerated people no longer live for the advantage of themselves but live for the advantage of Christ who died and rose again for us. We live for His benefit. Life's purpose is bound up with life's origin.

The words on my coffee mug remind me of my purpose.

Lord, I have nothing to do today but to please you!

2 CORINTHIANS 5:16-21

For this reason
16 Ὥστε

    We, ourselves, from now on, experience no one according to flesh

    ἡμεῖς ἀπὸ τοῦ νῦν οὐδένα οἴδαμεν κατὰ σάρκα·

    although we have experienced Christ according to flesh,

    εἰ καὶ ἐγνώκαμεν κατὰ σάρκα Χριστόν,

        but now no longer are we perceiving (him this way).

        ἀλλὰ νῦν οὐκέτι γινώσκομεν.

Therefore
17 ὥστε

    If anyone (is) in Christ, (he is) a new creation

    εἴ τις ἐν Χριστῷ, καινὴ κτίσις·

    the old things have ceased to exist, behold new things have come into existence.

    τὰ ἀρχαῖα παρῆλθεν, ἰδοὺ γέγονεν καινά.

Now all these things (are) from God
18 τὰ δὲ πάντα ἐκ τοῦ θεοῦ

    The one who reconciled us to Himself through Christ

    τοῦ καταλλάξαντος ἡμᾶς ἑαυτῷ διὰ Χριστοῦ

    and who entrusted to us the service of reconciliation,

    καὶ δόντος ἡμῖν τὴν διακονίαν τῆς καταλλαγῆς,

        as that God was in Christ reconciling the world to Himself,

        19 ὡς ὅτι θεὸς ἦν ἐν Χριστῷ κόσμον καταλλάσσων ἑαυτῷ,

            Not keeping a record against them of their wrongdoings

            μὴ λογιζόμενος αὐτοῖς τὰ παραπτώματα αὐτῶν

        and deposited in us the word of reconciliation

        καὶ θέμενος ἐν ἡμῖν τὸν λόγον τῆς καταλλαγῆς.

Therefore, on behalf of Christ we are ambassadors
20 Ὑπὲρ Χριστοῦ οὖν πρεσβεύομεν

        As though God is imploring through us

        ὡς τοῦ θεοῦ παρακαλοῦντος δι' ἡμῶν·

    we are pleading on behalf of Christ

    δεόμεθα ὑπὲρ Χριστοῦ,

        be reconciled to God.

        καταλλάγητε τῷ θεῷ.

the one who did not know sin by experience he caused to be sin on behalf of us.
21 τὸν μὴ γνόντα ἁμαρτίαν ὑπὲρ ἡμῶν ἁμαρτίαν ἐποίησεν,

    In order that we ourselves might come to be the righteousness of God in Him.

    ἵνα ἡμεῖς γενώμεθα δικαιοσύνη θεοῦ ἐν αὐτῷ.

PREACHING POINTS

Verse 21 could be taken as subordinate to verse 20. However, the editors of the Greek text placed a period after verse 20. The sentence in verse 21 is so theologically significant that it seems best to let it stand alone as a preaching point. This gives us five preaching points in the passage. These five preaching points are propositions explaining who we are in Christ. The big idea focuses on our identity in Christ.

Central Idea:

1. (vs. 16)

2. (vs. 17)

3. (vs. 18-19)

4. (vs. 20)

5. (vs. 21)

Briefly identify two contemporary life parallels to these verses.

CLP #1

CLP #2

HOW DO WE KNOW WHO WE KNOW?

Relationships are forever changed when we become Christians. We do not regard each other the same way in Christ as we did before Christ. Paul wrote: *"For this reason, we, from now on, know no one according to the flesh. Although we have known Christ according to the flesh, but now we no longer know Him in this way"* (2 Corinthians 5:16). The old order of life has passed. Earthly distinctions no longer matter. A new way of life began in Christ. We can no longer evaluate each other according to the worldly criteria of social status, achievements, or success. We must not bring those standards into the church because we have been changed.

DID PAUL KNOW JESUS DURING HIS EARTHLY MINISTRY? The word translated "although" literally means "even if" (εἰ καὶ). The condition is assumed to be true (RIEN, p.469). It is possible that Paul did see Jesus during His earthly ministry since he came to Jerusalem to study under Rabbi Gamaliel during his teen years when Jesus was alive (WITH, p.307; BRUC, p.43). Some have gone so far as to suggest that Paul might have been the rich young ruler who interviewed Jesus (HUGH, p.198). Whatever Paul's knowledge of the historical Jesus, he is drawing a sharp contrast between his former attitude toward Jesus and his current attitude toward Jesus (BRUC, p.99). The line separating the two attitudes cuts through the heart when anyone comes to Christ. We are forever changed by Christ to see Christ differently after regeneration.

WHAT DOES IT MEAN TO NO LONGER KNOW CHRIST ACCORDING TO THE FLESH? The prepositional phrase "according to the flesh" (κατὰ σάρκα) is adverbial, modifying the verb "have known" (ἐγνώκαμεν) not the noun "Christ" (Χριστόν). The way we know is according to the flesh or not according to the flesh (WITH, p.394). The standard for measuring our knowledge is fleshly or not fleshly. If we know Christ by the superficial standards of this world - who He is, what He did, what He said - we are no different than many. Crowds followed Jesus, but they did not know Jesus in a spiritually regenerate way. Many today claim to know Jesus because they know about Jesus, but to know about Jesus is not to know Jesus at all (HUGH, p.201). Our conversion changes how we know Christ. True Christians no longer know Christ by the superficial standards of the world. True Christians no longer know Christ "according to the flesh" (κατὰ σάρκα). We know Christ by "the Spirit of the Living God" (πνεύματι Θεοῦ ζῶντος, 2 Corinthians 3:3).

HOW DO WE KNOW NO ONE ACCORDING TO THE FLESH? Paul starts with this assertion. We evaluate others and are evaluated by others according to an entirely new standard of knowing. We no longer judge others or are judged by others according to the world's standards of success. Being in Christ changes how we relate to others in Christ. External, superficial, outward measurements should not determine how we relate to one another. Wealth, status, position, and achievement are not the yardsticks for our relationships in Christ. We know no one by these standards. We judge ministry by different standards as well. We died in Christ (2 Corinthians 5:14), so we live by the standards of the cross. The crucified life marks our relationships forever. We know who we know at the foot of the cross.

A NEW WORLD DAWNING

The dawn of a new world has broken over the horizon of darkness. We, Christians, are the vanguard of God's new creation which will someday wholly replace the old world order. Paul wrote, *Therefore, if anyone is in Christ, there is a new creation; the entire old order has passed away, behold the new has come to be* (2 Corinthians 5:17).

There is no verb in the opening clause so we must supply one. A common interpretation is to make this into a statement of personal regeneration. *If anyone is in Christ, he is a new creature.* The noun (κτίσις) can mean "creature," and it is certainly legitimate to supply "he is" as the verb. The verse would be understood as an explanation of regeneration. The form of the expression is similar to the Rabbinic language for proselyte conversion and the forgiveness of sins (MEY, p. 534). Paul uses similar language when he writes that we are *created* (κτισθέντες) *in Christ Jesus* (Eph. 2:10).

However, I think it best to understand the verse as speaking about a new creation that Christians inhabit when we are placed into Christ. Do the words "new creation" (καινὴ κτίσις) explain the person (anyone, τις) or "in Christ" (ἐν Χριστῷ)? The emphasis falls on "in Christ." The new creation defines "in Christ" more than personal regeneration (MART, p. 152). We become part of a new creation in Christ. The old world order has passed away for us, and we are now part of a whole new world that has dawned. We certainly must be new creatures (by regeneration) to be part of the new creation, but I think the emphasis is on what it means to be part of the new creation for three reasons.

1) The noun κτίσις is more commonly used for God's creation, whereas the noun κτίσμα is more commonly understood as creatures (NIDNTT, 1:378). James 1:18 says that *God brought us forth ... so that we would be a kind of firstfruits among His creatures* (κτισμάτων). The Qumran sect used the concept of a new creation (κτίσις) to refer to a new world order that the righteous would inhabit after the old world order disintegrated (NIDNTT, 1:383).

2) The following clause explains the new creation. Paul says *the old order has passed away.* The neuter plural adjective (τὰ ἀρχαῖα) means the total of everything old (ATR, p. 654). When combined with the verb "passed away" (παρῆλθεν), the sense refers to an old world order (MART, p. 534). The verb translated "passed away" is used elsewhere for the passing away of an old world order (HUGH, p. 203, fn 42). Peter uses this word in 2 Peter 3:10 to describe the Day of the Lord when the heavens will pass away (παρελεύσονται) with a roar (cf. Mt. 24:35). John uses a similar verb in Revelation 21:4 when he describes a world without death, mourning or pain because the first things have passed away (ἀπῆλθαν).

3) The opening word of the verse (ὥστε) ties verse 17 directly to verse 16. Verse 17 is the result of what he has said in verse 16. Our relationships with one another and with Christ have been completely changed because we are part of a whole new creation. We no longer recognize others according to our physical connections, but we relate to one another in a new and spiritual way. The prejudices of the old world have passed away in this new creation. In Christ, we practice a new way of relating to others because we are part of a new creation.

A new world order is dawning. Because we are new creations in Christ, we are part of a new creation of Christ. One day we will see the new world in all its glory. We will see *a new heaven and a new earth for the first heaven and the first earth have passed away* (ἀπῆλθαν). We will finally and fully experience our new creation relationships with God and with others in ways we can only glimpse today (Revelation 21:1-4). Awesome!

THE MINISTRY OF RECONCILIATION

To reconcile is to make peace, to bring an end to hostility. We live in a hostile world. The root of that hostility is bound up in man's rebellion against God, which leads to hostility towards others. Paul wrote, *Now all these things* (the new creation, vs.17) *are from God who reconciled us to Himself through Christ and who gave to us the ministry of reconciliation, that is God was in Christ reconciling the world to Himself, not counting against them their sins, and having deposited in us the word of reconciliation* (2 Cor. 5:18-19).

Reconciliation begins with God and ends with man. God is no helpless victim of man's hostility. The hostility goes both directions. Humans rebelled against God, and God is angry at humans. If we do not take the wrath of God seriously, then the cross becomes a cruel and unjust exercise of a petty deity. God, on the cross, poured out His wrath upon Christ to reconcile us to Himself (HUGH, p.205). God takes the initiative in reconciliation. The verb translated "reconciled" (καταλλάξαντος) is in the active voice. Paul always uses the active voice of this verb to indicate God's actions while the passive voice indicates our response. God reconciles us. We are reconciled to God (WITH, p.396, fn. 14). The voice of the verb is theologically important. We cannot reconcile ourselves to God. Only God can reconcile us to Himself because only He can remove His hostility toward us.

The structure of these two verses in the Greek text is significant. God made peace with us by not counting against us our sins. How? He made peace with us because Jesus became sin for us (v.21). The cross is the foundation for our ministry of reconciliation. Vertical peace with God precedes horizontal peace with others. The cross is the basis for all peacemaking on earth.

God reconciled us to Himself through Christ
          and gave to us the ministry of reconciliation
God was in Christ reconciling the world to Himself
          not counting against them their sins
               and having deposited in us the word of reconciliation.

Two parallel clauses describe our peacemaking service in this world. God gave, and God deposited. God gave (δόντος) to us the ministry of reconciliation. God acted unilaterally to remove His hostility toward us by paying for it on the cross. Reconciliation is His gift to us, so the ministry of reconciliation is also His gift to us (NIDNTT, 3:166). Ministry or service (διακονίαν) is a gift even as it is a deposit. God deposited (θέμενος) in us the word of reconciliation. The verb translated "deposited" is an Aorist participle of the verb τίθημι which means to put, place, or lay something (BAGD, p.815). God put in us the word of reconciliation.

The ministry (διακονίαν) and the word (λόγον) are parallel. The ministry of reconciliation consists of the word of reconciliation. We announce peace. We proclaim the end of hostility. We speak reconciliation. As has often been said, the gospel is not good advice. It is good news. Our job is to announce the good news. We must be careful not to turn the good news into bad news by adding qualifiers to the word of reconciliation deposited in our lives. Our lives should reflect the reconciliation we received.

Vertical peace with God paves the way for horizontal peace with others. Paul is writing to a divided and conflicted church. The Christians were quarreling with each other and with him. Such fights are inconsistent with Christianity. We are given the ministry of peace talking. Peace talking is deposited in our lives. We are called to be peace talkers. The ministry of reconciliation is inextricably bound up in the apostolic preaching of the cross. We cannot, at the same time, announce peace with God while living in enmity with men!

RECONCILING THE WORLD

Reconciliation is a two-way street. God must reconcile us to Himself, and we must be reconciled to Him. There is enmity between God and man, which goes both directions. Our rebellion against God must be reconciled, and God's anger toward us must be reconciled. Paul writes that *"God was reconciling the world to Himself in Christ"* (2 Cor. 5:19) and then concludes with an appeal to *"be reconciled to God"* (2 Cor. 5:20). The compound verb translated "reconcile" (καταλλάσσων) is perfective meaning to effect a complete change back from enmity to peace (MHT, 3:298). Reconciliation is not complete until both sides are reconciled.

Paul is the only one who uses the verb καταλλάσσω for the relationship between God and man. The active voice is only used of God, and the passive voice is only used for humans (TDNT, 1:255). We do not achieve reconciliation with God. Reconciliation with God is never something we can accomplish. To imply otherwise is to deny the gospel - the good news of what God has done for us (MART, p. 154).

In Christ, God was reconciling the world "to Himself" (ἑαυτῷ). God pacified Himself in Christ. The sacrifice of the Son appeased the anger of the Father. Paul writes, "while we were enemies we were reconciled (κατηλλάγημεν) to God through the death of His Son" (Rom. 5:10). God made peace with Himself for us so that no impediment stood between Him and us any longer. He reconciled (active voice); we were reconciled (passive voice)! He did it for us! This is the essence of the good news.

When Paul writes that God *"was reconciling the world to Himself"* (2 Cor. 5:19), he was not suggesting universalism. The present tense of the verb (καταλλάσσων) indicates continuous, ongoing reconciliation. The "world" (κόσμον) refers to a class of people. The absence of an article gives the noun a collective sense. He is referring to humanity as a whole. God is "not imputing to them" (αὐτοῖς) "their" (αὐτῶν) "sins." The plural pronouns refer back to a collective singular (BD, p.147). The individual members of the collective world are being reconciled to God down through history.

Paul does not mean that all humans, believing and unbelieving, are forgiven, but God, in Christ, forgives the sins of those who are part of the collective world (HOD, 145). Imputation was sufficient for the whole world but efficient only in Christ. The cross was sufficient to remove the judicial anger on God's side, but it does not remove the rebellion on our side of reconciliation.

Humans must receive the reconciliation to be reconciled. We must accept what God has done for us before reconciliation is complete for both sides.

How else can we understand Paul's appeal to "be reconciled to God" (2 Cor. 5:21)? The verb is in the passive voice. We appeal to humans to be reconciled (καταλλάγητε) to God. Humans don't reconcile themselves to God. Humans accept the reconciliation God has made for them by turning away from their rebellion to enjoy peace with God. God commissions us to urge people to receive the reconciliation provided by God. The Gospel is good news because we declare what God has done, not what we must do to be reconciled to God!

AMBASSADORS FOR PEACE

Our mission is the ministry of reconciliation (2 Cor. 5:18). God reconciled us to Himself in Christ, *"therefore, we are ambassadors for Christ, as though God were making an appeal through us; we beg you on behalf of Christ, be reconciled to God"* (2 Cor. 5:20).

The word translated "ambassadors" (πρεσβεύομεν) is a verb, not a noun. Originally, the verb meant to be the oldest or to assume first place in rank. By the time of Paul, the verb came to mean the actions of an ambassador who represents another person in negotiations (NIDNTT, 1:193). The word was used to refer to the Emperor's legate, one who carries out the official duties of an envoy or emissary. Those duties could include petition and intercession on behalf of the king (MM, p.534). Paul uses the same verb to describe his mission in Ephesians 6:20, where he writes, *"I am an ambassador in chains"* (πρεσβεύω ἐν ἁλύσει). Chains may become the badge of our position because we represent a king, not of this world.

We act as representatives not just on behalf of Christ but in place of Christ (ὑπὲρ Χριστοῦ). The prepositional phrase is placed first in the sentence for emphasis. It is true that the preposition ὑπὲρ does not necessarily infer a substitutionary meaning like the preposition ἀντὶ. However, ὑπὲρ is often used in a vicarious way meaning "instead of" or "in place of" someone else, and the context here supports such a substitutionary meaning (HUGH, p.209, fn 48, see p.193, fn 24). We are ambassadors in place of Jesus Christ, which is why when we speak we are speaking *"as though God were making an appeal through us."* The particle ὡς followed by the genitive absolute τοῦ θεοῦ makes the genitive the subject of the participle παρακαλοῦντος (RIEN, p.470). The better translation would read: "We are ambassadors in place of Christ, with the conviction that God is appealing through us." When we as His ambassadors talk peace, God talks through us. God is present in our words (MART, p.156).

Our mission is to call all people to *"be reconciled to God"* (καταλλάγητε τῷ θεῷ). Paul does not say that we call people to believe they are reconciled. We plead with people to be reconciled (WITH, p.397, fn 16). People are to put away the enmity in their hearts toward God (repentance) by accepting God's peace achieved for them in Christ (faith). God appeals (παρακαλοῦντος) to people through us. The verb means to implore, entreat, or request people to be reconciled (BAGD, p.617).

The appeal to be vertically reconciled to God leads naturally into the appeal to be horizontally reconciled to each other. Paul is not only thinking of the outside world in this appeal. He is thinking about the Corinthians themselves as the following verses make clear. He is concerned that the professing Christians in Corinth might have received the grace of God in vain according to the next verse (2 Cor. 6:1) so he urges or appeals (παρακαλοῦμεν) to them to be reconciled. Later he will beg them to *"make room for him in their hearts"* (2 Cor. 7:2-4). Paul sees the dynamic connection between vertical and horizontal reconciliation.

We are ambassadors for peace in a hostile world. No peace with God means no peace with others. No peace with others is a sign we have no peace with God. God talks peace when we talk peace! Lord, help me to be a peacemaker for you.

THE PRICE OF PEACE

The clearest and most important verse in the Bible regarding justification is 2 Corinthians 5:21. God made peace with us by removing the enmity between us, but someone must pay to reconcile enemies. Forensic payment for sin is justification. Paul writes, *"Be reconciled to God. The one who knew no sin, He made to be sin on our behalf, in order that we might become the righteousness of God in Him."*

Verse 21 is an example of asyndeton, a sentence that is grammatically unconnected to what comes before or after (MHT, 3:340). Paul's transition from the topic of reconciliation to justification is abrupt without any connecting particles. The verse stands alone grammatically but is essential to the overall argument Paul advances. To be reconciled requires us to be justified.

God made (ἐποίησεν) the sinless Christ to be sin for us. Christ is sin. He is neither sinner nor sin offering. Christ is sin (ἁμαρτία), not a sinner (ἁμαρτωλός). This point is important theologically for if Christ became a sinner, He could not die for our sins. God made him sin itself, the object of God's forensic anger so that our sin could be judged and removed. Reconciliation depends on the removal of that which caused God to be angry by the satisfying of His judicial wrath. Furthermore, Christ is not merely a sin offering like the scapegoat under the Mosaic law. We discern this truth because of the double use of the noun "sin" which requires us to take both uses of sin in the same way. While it is possible to understand "he made Him sin" as "He made him a sin offering," it is not possible to take "the one who knew no sin" as "the one who knew no sin offering." Therefore both uses of the word must mean sin, not sin offering (HUGH, pp. 213-215).

The two clauses are parallel. Paul draws a sharp contrast between sin (ἁμαρτίαν) and righteousness (δικαιοσύνη) and between made (ἐποίησεν) and might become (γενώμεθα). Christ was made sin. We are not made righteous. Our righteousness is a gift of God in Christ. It is the righteousness of God (θεοῦ) which must be understood as a subjective genitive meaning that the righteousness comes from God. It is also only a righteousness found in Him (ἐν αὐτῷ). The antecedent must be Christ (Χριστοῦ) in verse 20. God gives us His righteousness because of our union with Christ.

Since righteousness is a gift from God (Rom. 5:17), it cannot mean good works. Good works cannot be given to us. The righteousness Paul is talking about must refer to a right relationship with God. God confers a standing of righteousness on us in Christ. God provides the right standing Christ bought for us. The gift is judicial righteousness on the basis of His payment for sin. In this sense, our sin is imputed to Christ, and His right standing with God is imputed to us (MOR, pp.281-282).

God both requires of us and provides to us His righteousness. The verb "might become" (γενώμεθα) infers a growing life of actual righteousness (good works) as the result of this conferral of judicial righteousness (Eph. 2:10) although Paul's emphasis is forensic in this passage.

Reconciliation depends on justification, and justification depends on atonement. Justification is judicial forgiveness. Christ paid the price for God to forgive. Because God forgives, we can be reconciled to God and offer reconciliation to others. The price tag of peace is payment for sins.

2 CORINTHIANS 6:1-7:4

2 CORINTHIANS 6:1-10

Now working together (with God cf. 5:20)

Συνεργοῦντες δὲ

We also are imploring you not to accept the grace of God without result

καὶ παρακαλοῦμεν μὴ εἰς κενὸν τὴν χάριν τοῦ θεοῦ δέξασθαι ὑμᾶς·

for He says, At the appropriate time I answered

2 λέγει γάρ· καιρῷ δεκτῷ ἐπήκουσά σου

and in the day of salvation I helped you.

καὶ ἐν ἡμέρᾳ σωτηρίας ἐβοήθησά σοι.

Behold now (is) the suitable time,

ἰδοὺ νῦν καιρὸς εὐπρόσδεκτος,

behold now is the day of salvation.

ἰδοὺ νῦν ἡμέρα σωτηρίας.

Giving no one in nothing an obstacle,

3 Μηδεμίαν ἐν μηδενὶ διδόντες προσκοπήν,

In order that no blame might be found in the ministry,

ἵνα μὴ μωμηθῇ ἡ διακονία,

but in everything recommending ourselves as servants of God,

4 ἀλλ᾽ ἐν παντὶ συνιστάντες ἑαυτοὺς ὡς θεοῦ διάκονοι,

By much perseverance,

ἐν ὑπομονῇ πολλῇ,

in pressures, in troubles, in distresses,

ἐν θλίψεσιν, ἐν ἀνάγκαις, ἐν στενοχωρίαις,

in beatings, in jails, in mobs,

5 ἐν πληγαῖς, ἐν φυλακαῖς, ἐν ἀκαταστασίαις,

In hard labors, in sleepless nights, in starvations,

ἐν κόποις, ἐν ἀγρυπνίαις, ἐν νηστείαις,

by sincerity, by knowledge, by patience, by kindness,

6 ἐν ἁγνότητι, ἐν γνώσει, ἐν μακροθυμίᾳ, ἐν χρηστότητι,

by the Holy Spirit, by authentic love,

ἐν πνεύματι ἁγίῳ, ἐν ἀγάπῃ ἀνυποκρίτῳ,

by a truthful message, by the power of God

7 ἐν λόγῳ ἀληθείας, ἐν δυνάμει θεοῦ·

Through the weapons of righteousness for the right and left hands

διὰ τῶν ὅπλων τῆς δικαιοσύνης τῶν δεξιῶν καὶ ἀριστερῶν,

through fame and disgrace, through slander and praise

8 διὰ δόξης καὶ ἀτιμίας, διὰ δυσφημίας καὶ εὐφημίας·

As deceiving and truthful, as unknown and well recognized,

ὡς πλάνοι καὶ ἀληθεῖς, **9** ὡς ἀγνοούμενοι καὶ ἐπιγινωσκόμενοι,

as dying and behold we are alive, as being punished and not executed,

ὡς ἀποθνήσκοντες καὶ ἰδοὺ ζῶμεν, ὡς παιδευόμενοι καὶ μὴ θανατούμενοι,

as grieving and yet rejoicing, as poor yet enriching many,

10 ὡς λυπούμενοι ἀεὶ δὲ χαίροντες, ὡς πτωχοὶ πολλοὺς δὲ πλουτίζοντες,

As possessing nothing and owning everything.

ὡς μηδὲν ἔχοντες καὶ πάντα κατέχοντες.

PREACHING POINTS

The United Bible Society text treats all ten verses as one sentence. The Nestle/Aland text (seen here) places a period at the end of verse two, and the rest of the passage is a single sentence. In either case, the main subject and predicate in this passage are "we" and "are imploring you not to accept the grace of God without result" in verse one. This sentence is the central idea. There are three preaching points explaining how we avoid receiving the grace of God in vain or emptiness.

Central Idea:

1. (vs. 1-2)

2. (vs. 3)

3. (vs. 4-10)

Briefly identify two contemporary life parallels to these verses.

CLP #1

CLP #2

EMPTY RECONCILIATION

What does it mean to receive the grace of God in vain? Paul wrote in 2 Corinthians 6:1, "And working together; we also are appealing to you not in vain to receive the grace of God." The words conclude Paul's explanation of God's reconciling work in Christ and the reconciling ministry we have toward others (2 Cor. 5:16-21). Therefore, Paul warns us not to receive God's grace in vain.

The infinitive "to receive" (δέξασθαι) means to receive a gift from someone or to receive someone into your home (BAGD, p.177). Paul uses the word in 2 Corinthians 7:15 to describe the reception the Corinthian church gave to Titus, his messenger. The negative particle (μὴ) goes with the infinitive rather than the verb "appeal" (παρακαλοῦμεν) because οὐκ is used with indicatives while μὴ is used with the other moods (BAGD, p.590). The sense is "we appeal to you not to receive" as opposed to "we do not appeal to you to receive." The phrase translated "in vain" (εἰς κενὸν) means without result, without reaching its goal. God's grace is empty and achieves no purpose (BAGD, p.427) if it is received in vain.

Is it even possible to receive the grace of God in a way that proves to be ineffective? Philip Hughes raises that question and then summarizes the four ways that this phrase is interpreted (HUGH, pp.217-219). 1) Paul is talking about receiving God's grace in a purely external and superficial manner. Such a person is a professing Christian but not a true believer. However, the context makes it unlikely that Paul is talking about false professions of faith. 2) Paul is talking about a person who accepts God's grace only to reject it later. Such a person loses his salvation, thus receiving the grace in vain. This view flies in the face of Paul's statements elsewhere regarding salvation (e.g., Phil. 1:6) 3) Paul's appeal is not directed toward the Corinthians but to the world in general to whom God offers His reconciliation. Paul appeals to the world not to reject this great salvation. In this view, people do not receive the grace in vain. They never receive it all. 4) Paul is talking about Christians when they stand before the Judgment Seat of Christ (2 Cor. 5:10)

The best interpretation is the fourth view. To receive the grace of God in vain is to live in ways that are inconsistent with grace. Our practice does not match our doctrine. Here we go back to the meaning of the word "vain" (κενὸν) above. The grace of God does not produce the intended results in our lives. Our actions constitute a denial of the truth. When we stand before Christ's judgment seat (the evaluation of believers not unbelievers), our actions will prove to be empty of eternal value. The purifying fire of God's judgment will consume the wood, hay, and stubble in our lives, although we will be saved "as through fire" (1 Cor. 3:10-15).

Paul writes these words in the context of a great parenthesis in his letter (2 Cor. 2:14 - 7:4) dealing with sin and conflict in the body. He exhorts them to forgive the sinful offender before the parenthesis and then commends them for that forgiveness after the parenthesis (2 Cor. 2:7, cf. 2 Cor. 7:12). The conflict includes Paul, who has felt alienated from the people in Corinth (2:2:13, cf. 7:5-16). Reconciliation is meant to transform our relationships. If we are reconciled to God by His grace, then we should be reconciled to one another as well. If we are not reconciled with one another, then we have received God's grace in vain. In this case, His reconciling grace serves no purpose in our lives (MART, p.166).

Horizontal reconciliation proves we have not received vertical reconciliation in vain!

DO NO HARM

How often do we "bag it" and move on in our relationships with other Christians? Disagreements, irritations, and hurt feelings develop. We distance ourselves from one another, dismissing the relationships as peripheral to ministry. Not Paul! He writes, *"working together we also urge you ... giving no cause for offense at all that the ministry might not be blemished"* (2 Cor. 6:1&3). The first rule of ministry, like medicine, is to do no harm.

Paul spoke his letters like a pastor preaching to his people. One feature of oral communication is anacoluthon, a dramatic break in the sentence structure so that the final thought does not follow grammatically from the previous thought (ATR, p.435). Anacoluthon shows the depth of emotion that Paul feels as he breaks into his own sentence with a new thought in verse three. The phrase "giving" (διδόντες) no offense skips over verse 2 and qualifies or explains "we urge you" (παρακαλοῦμεν) in verse 1 (MEY, p. 546). What follows (vs. 4-10) is a long list of emotional experiences that Paul uses to appeal to the affections of the Corinthians before he concludes his appeal with his "heart opened wide" to them (vs. 11).

Paul starts his anacoluthon with an emphatic double negative (μηδεμίαν ἐν μηδενὶ), meaning "no offense at all" (RIEN, p.471). The participle "giving" (διδόντες) is in the present tense indicating ongoing, continuous action. Giving no offense at all is not a one-time act but a habit of life. In ministry, we are constantly seeking to give no offense to others - to do no harm in the church. The word "offense" (προσκοπήν) is only used here in the New Testament and means "an occasion for making a misstep" (BAGD, p.716). It is related to the more common word (πρόσκομμα) meaning an obstacle or hindrance, referring to the stumbling itself.

Paul wants to give no reason for anyone to stumble so that "the ministry might not be discredited" (μωμηθῇ). The verb means to find fault with or to blame. The noun form (μῶμος) means a defect or a blemish, and Peter uses it as a description of false teachers in 2 Peter 2:13 (BAGD, p.531). The noun is frequently used in the book of Leviticus to describe defects or blemishes in the sacrifices of the priests (HR, 2:93). No priest, for example, could come near to the altar to offer a sacrifice if he had a blemish (Lev. 21:21). Our ministries today are not discredited by physical blemishes but by spiritual blemishes. If we cause offense to others, we blemish our ministries. At the very least, we should do no harm to the church always seeking her interest instead of our self-interests in all our decisions.

Paul is beginning his final emotional appeal to the Corinthians to be reconciled to him (WITH, p.398). He is writing to believers who have become estranged from him. He pleads with them to open their hearts - their affections - to him as he has to them (6:11-13). Paul is wearing his heart on his sleeve as he extends his hand to them in reconciliation. He does not want to be the cause of anything that blemishes his relationship with them in the ministry of Jesus Christ.

Relationships matter in ministry!

THE PREACHER'S ETHOS

Perched precariously on our shaky pedestals, we preachers can feel vulnerable to the changing tides of popularity. The lure of pragmatism - using rhetorical methods to generate crowds - is powerful, especially when critics blame our lack of success on methodological failure. Paul dealt with the rhetorical sophists of his day in 2 Corinthians. His letter is an example of "forensic rhetoric" (WITH, p.333ff). Forensic rhetoric was the use of rhetoric to defend the communicator. Paul develops his proposition (*propositio* in forensic rhetoric) in 2 Corinthians 2:17. "For we are not like many, peddling the Word of God, but as from sincerity, but as from God, we speak in Christ in the sight of God." Here is the proposition Paul is defending in his letter (WITH, p.371).

There were three categories of classical rhetoric, logos, ethos, and pathos. Ethos referred to the character of the preacher. Paul defends his character as a preacher in 2 Corinthians 6. The structure of 2 Corinthians 6:1-4 helps us understand his defense. The main verb is "we urge" or "we appeal" (παρακαλοῦμεν, v.1). It is followed by two parallel participles explaining the preaching appeal: "giving" (διδόντες, v.3) no cause for offense and "commending" (συνίσταντες, v.4) ourselves as "servants of God." Both are present tense participles indicating continuous action.

Paul asks a question immediately following his proposition 2 Corinthians 2:17. "Are we beginning to commend ourselves again?" (3:1) The verb "to commend" (συνίστημι) comes from two words meaning "to put or place" (ἵστημι) and "with someone" (σύν). The classical sense of the verb grew out of the meaning to "stand together" leading to the idea of commendation (TDNT, 7:896-898). Paul says that we who are appealing are commending ourselves to you. The nominative case connects the participle to the subject of the main verb.

How does Paul commend himself to the Corinthians? He defends his ethos, his character. In classical rhetoric, the most powerfully persuasive arguments came from personal integrity - ethos! So we, like Paul, commend ourselves as "servants of God." The word "servants" (διάκονοι) is a nominative plural to agree with the subject "we." Paul is saying, "as servants of God, we commend ourselves" (ATR, p.454). It is who we are not what we do. We are not recommending ourselves to be servants as if interviewing for the role. We preachers are already servants which is the basis for our recommendation of ourselves to others. Our primary ethical qualification for ministry is servanthood.

Paul has been deeply hurt and discouraged by the criticisms of the Corinthians. He is seeking reconciliation with them. They have criticized him for his failure to be successful as a Greek rhetor (speaker), and he is defending his character as an apostle from those who claim he is a failure. We, too, face our critics whenever we are not as successful as other preachers by the standards of pragmatism. How do we defend ourselves from those attacks? We defend ourselves by arguing that we are not peddlers of the Word of God selling our wares to consumers. We are servants of God. Our ethos is our defense. Servanthood is the way we recommend ourselves. It is the foundation of our commendation. Servanthood is our ethos - our character - in ministry.

MONUMENTS OF SERVICE

Paul was tough. The list of sufferings in 2 Corinthians 6:4-10 boggles the mind. Chrysostom called Paul's CV a "blizzard of troubles" (MART, p.172). Most of us want our CVs to be more self-promoting, not Paul. He repeated a similar list of his qualifications for ministry in 2 Corinthians 11:21-27 (cf. 4:7-11) to show that true ministry is demonstrated by sacrifice.

The Greek text of 2 Corinthians 6:4-10 shows great emotion. Paul was so passionate about his list of struggles that he used grammar loosely to share his heart (MOU, p.196) as if his words flowed faster than his scribe could pen. Sacrifice marks our service in the cause of Christ. We are foot soldiers in the army of His kingdom.

Battle scars are the marks of ministry. Paul shares with pride his wounds representing the stigmata which prove him to be the slave of Christ (BRUC, p.462). He boasts about his hardships (2 Corinthians 11:30), something we rarely do today. But Paul is not boasting to promote himself. He takes pains to avoid self-promotion. His CV is for ministry promotion. He does it to defend the ministry.

We moderns find this boasting offensive, but in a culture built around honor and shame, this was an acceptable model for ministry defense. Paul knew the rules of rhetoric for what was considered "inoffensive self-praise," and he used those rhetorical tools well (WITH2, p.300). The list is similar to a list in Tacitus. The Stoics and the Cynics used lists like this to demonstrate character, so it was a well-established method for personal defense (WITH, p.399). Paul is defending his apostolic ministry with this resume of hardships.

The rhetorical structure of the passage breaks down into three general themes. 1) Hardships in service prove his endurance (4b-5). 2) Virtues of character prove his integrity (6-7a). Tools from God prove his wisdom (7b-10). First, Paul uses nine phrases grouped in threes and introduced by "in much endurance" (ἐν ὑπομονῇ πολλῇ). Each phrase begins with the same preposition "in" (ἐν) to show that our endurance in ministry is demonstrated in hardships. Next, Paul uses eight phrases which are also introduced by the preposition "in" (ἐν) in verses 6-7a. The virtues demonstrate that Paul handled the hardships of ministry with integrity. Paul is demonstrating his ethos with this list. The greatest test of our integrity is how we handle adversity. Finally, Paul uses phrases to show that God has equipped him with the tools to live wisely. There are three phrases introduced by the preposition "through" (διὰ) and seven phrases introduced by the comparative "as" (ὡς).

Paul is raising the bar for evaluating ministry. Our qualifications for ministry revolve around the model of the cross. The Corinthians were enamored with the world's wisdom of success and power and forgetting Christ's wisdom of the cross and suffering. The wise life with Christ is the life of suffering, not success (WITH, pp.398-401).

We live in a day when self-promotion, marketing, and savvy media methods grow many ministries. Paul would not say that we are wrong to use accepted cultural methods (modern media) because he used the accepted rhetorical practices of his day. However, Paul lays out a refreshing model for ministry promotion emphasizing sacrifice and suffering. Sacrificial service leaves scars which are the monuments of ministry worth remembering.

101

2 CORINTHIANS 6:11-13 AND 7:2-4

Our mouth has been completely open with you,
11 Τὸ στόμα ἡμῶν ἀνέῳγεν πρὸς ὑμᾶς,
Corinthians
Κορίνθιοι,
Our heart has been enlarged
ἡ καρδία ἡμῶν πεπλάτυνται·
You are not cramped by us,
12 οὐ στενοχωρεῖσθε ἐν ἡμῖν,
But you are cramped in your feelings
στενοχωρεῖσθε δὲ ἐν τοῖς σπλάγχνοις ὑμῶν·
now the same exchange,
13 τὴν δὲ αὐτὴν ἀντιμισθίαν,
I speak as to little children,
ὡς τέκνοις λέγω,
You, yourselves, also enlarge (your hearts)
πλατύνθητε καὶ ὑμεῖς.

Make space for us
2 Χωρήσατε ἡμᾶς·
We have harmed no one,
οὐδένα ἠδικήσαμεν,
we have ruined no one
οὐδένα ἐφθείραμεν,
we have manipulated no one.
οὐδένα ἐπλεονεκτήσαμεν.
I do not speak in order to condemn
3 πρὸς κατάκρισιν οὐ λέγω·
For I have said before
προείρηκα γὰρ
that you are in our hearts
ὅτι ἐν ταῖς καρδίαις ἡμῶν ἐστε
to die with and to live with.
εἰς τὸ συναποθανεῖν καὶ συζῆν.
Great for my part (is) frankness to you,
4 πολλή μοι παρρησία πρὸς ὑμᾶς,
Great for my part (is boasting on behalf of you
πολλή μοι καύχησις ὑπὲρ ὑμῶν·
I have been filled up with encouragement
πεπλήρωμαι τῇ παρακλήσει,
I am superabounding with joy
ὑπερπερισσεύομαι τῇ χαρᾷ
in regard to all our trouble.
ἐπὶ πάσῃ τῇ θλίψει ἡμῶν.

PREACHING POINTS

The enlarging our hearts (6:11&13) and the making room or space in our hearts for others (7:2-3) tie these two passages together. The verses in between (6:14-7:1) form an important and unified parenthesis in Paul's argument. For these reasons, it is best to treat 6:11-13 and 7:2-4 as one unit of thought for preaching purposes. The big idea focuses on affections and relationships. There are four preaching points which form the principles for understanding the renewal of our relationships with one another in Christ.

Central Idea:

1. (vs. 11-13)

2. (vs. 2)

3. (vs. 3)

4. (vs. 4)

Briefly identify two contemporary life parallels to these verses.

CLP #1

CLP #2

RECONCILIATION: CROSSING THE BRIDGE

Reconciliation requires us to be open with our feelings where once we were closed. When another has hurt us, we pull up the drawbridge to the castle of our hearts. We fill the moat with water to keep people away. The other party must cross the great divide to reach us. Crossing that bridge is an emotional challenge for all of us.

Paul had been deeply hurt in ministry. He was estranged from the Corinthians because of past feelings. His wounds were so deep that they affected his ministry, causing him to write this extended parenthesis of pain (2 Cor. 2:14-7:4). Paul models for us how we can attempt to cross the bridge of hard feelings. Paul writes, "Our mouth is open to you, Corinthians, our heart has been opened wide. ... Open wide to us also" (2 Cor. 6:11-13).

One side in a conflict must take the initiative to cross the bridge. Often what happens is that we say something like, "I'll forgive him if he forgives me." "She's got to take the first step. The ball is in her court." "If he reaches out to me, I'll work it out with him." Waiting means that reconciliation never takes place. We can stay in waiting mode for a very long time. Reconciliation requires that one person takes the initiative to walk across the bridge - to risk rejection to start the process.

Paul risks rejection. He uses two different words for "open" in verse 11. The first word for "open" (ἀνέῳγεν) refers to his mouth. If the mouth does not open, reconciliation never happens. The other person cannot know what is in my head unless I open my mouth. C.K. Barrett expresses it this way. "I have let my tongue run away with me" (BARR, p.191). Paul is referring to the previous verses, where he has talked about his sacrificial suffering. He is saying that he has freely spoken to them. He has not held back his feelings. There are no secrets. His mouth is an open book sharing his raw feelings for them (NIDNTT, 2:727). Huge risk! We do not know how the other party will react when we speak freely about our feelings. I may be rejected, but I must take that risk. I must cross the bridge.

The word is a perfect passive verb from ἀνοίγω. Paul says, "our mouth had been opened to you." He has opened his mouth in the previous chapters and freely shared his feelings. The open mouth has continuing results as he seeks reconciliation. The passive voice indicates that God influenced him to open his mouth. Sharing our feelings with one who has hurt us is not natural. God must open our mouths to do it.

Paul goes on to say that "our heart has been opened wide." The heart (καρδία) is the center of man where God is at work. The center of the inner man includes our will and our understanding. The heart is also the seat of our emotions (TDNT, 3:111-112). We use the heart as the seat of our emotions today. Paul is saying our inner man, including our feelings, has been opened wide. He uses a different verb for "open" (πεπλάτυνται) in this clause. It is the perfect passive of πλατύνω meaning to widen or enlarge. The noun (πλάτος) means the breadth or width of something. The enemies of God will come up on the "broad plain" (τὸ πλάτος τῆς γῆς) from the four corners of the earth to surround Jerusalem before God destroys them (Rev. 20:9). The verb was used for opening large leather cases that contained texts (NIDNTT, 1:253-254). Paul's heart was opened to them by God like a broad plain or the opening of a large briefcase.

Paul takes the initiative to cross the bridge and then appeals to them to "Open wide also" (πλατύνθητε). He uses an imperative, a command, but he softens it with the passive voice. "Let God through our appeal to you open wide your hearts to us like a broad plain." Reconciliation is a two-way street. The other side must allow their hearts to be opened wide so that their feelings are shared freely too. The bridge of alienation must be crossed in both directions to have true reconciliation - the open, free, and honest sharing of our feelings with one another.

Lord, help me to seek and accept reconciliation with my brothers and sisters in the church.

BEING VULNERABLE

When we've been hurt, it is hard to risk being vulnerable. I know that I tend to close the door to my feelings and put out the no trespassing sign. I put up walls to protect my heart. Paul shows us another way. Ministry calls for transparency and transparency can be traumatic. *"You are not being cramped by us,"* Paul wrote, *"but you are being cramped in your feelings. Now, in exchange, I am talking as little children, be opened wide to us also"* (2 Cor. 6:12-13).

Twice Paul uses an interesting word translated being cramped or restricted. The noun form of the word is a synonym for distress or affliction. The verb used here (στενοχωρεῖσθε) refers to a narrow space, being confined by inner or outer troubles. It means to be crowded, cramped, confined, or oppressed (NIDNTT, 2:807). Both verbs are in the present tense indicating ongoing action. The emotional constriction in their relationship was continuous. Paul assures them that he is not oppressing their emotions, but they are confining their emotions toward him. We oppress our feelings as a coping mechanism to avoid risking more rejection. If we open up and let our feelings be seen, we risk being hurt again. God urges us to open up anyway. Take the risk. Fear of rejection, like fear of failure, can cripple our ministries.

The noun translated "affections" or "feelings" (σπλάγχνοις) literally means "inward parts" or "entrails." It was specifically used for the more valuable parts of the sacrificial animal such as heart, lungs, liver, spleen, and kidneys. These organs were removed immediately after killing the animal and eaten as part of the sacrificial meal. In Greek culture, the word was used for the male sexual organs and the womb, so children were sometimes called σπλάγχνα because they were born from one's flesh and blood (NIDNTT, 2:599). As a result, people thought of the intestines as the seat of human passion. After all, we feel the physical effects of anger, sadness, and happiness in our abdomens. Our feelings are visceral!

The opening clause of verse 13 talks of an exchange of feelings. The noun (ἀντιμισθίαν) means a reward or penalty (BAGD, p.75). It may have been an expression made up by Paul, where he used a noun in an adverbial phrase by blending two more common expressions (MOU, p.160). The word itself is a compound noun with the preposition αντί (instead of) combined with the noun μισθός (reward) to express the thought of reciprocation (TDNT, 4:695-702). Paul encouraged the responsiveness of emotions. He shared his feelings and desired for them to share their feelings in return. The addition of the preposition αντί to the noun emphasizes the idea of exchange (NIDNTT, 3:197). An exchange of reward, a reciprocation of feelings, must take place between two people seeking reconciliation.

Lord, help me not to wall up my feelings, but to open my heart and risk rejection to build healthy relationships with my brothers and sisters in Christ.

FENCES FOR PERSUASIVE PASTORS

Paul has been pulling out all the persuasive stops in 2 Corinthians 6. He has worn his heart on his sleeve as he pleads with the Corinthians to open wide their hearts to him. Paul lays out his sacrificial love for them in a heart-tugging list of sufferings culminating in his emotional plea for their love (6:4-13). He concludes his powerful appeal by saying, "Make room for us in your hearts; we wronged no one, we corrupted no one, we took advantage of no one" (7:3).

As pastors, we are spiritual leaders whose goal is "moving people on to God's agenda" (BLACK). God uses pastors to persuade people to reconcile broken relationships as we follow the Lord together (2 Cor. 5:18). Pastoral leadership is all about influencing others. In this case, Paul wants to persuade them to "make room" (Χωρήσατε) for him in their hearts.

They say that fences make good neighbors. Fences also make good pastors. Since pastoral persuasion is moving people to follow God's will, God places ethical boundaries on our persuasion. These fences ensure that Pastors will submit their persuasive methods to God's sovereign control. We dare not manipulate others for our own ends or else we deny our Lord by our actions.

Paul lays out three fences in this verse to guard against unethical influence. He uses three verbs. Each verb is aorist, active indicative. They are best understood as constative aorists. Paul is saying that their ongoing actions in each case have been completed and should be regarded as a whole (BD, 171). The plural pronoun (we) likely included Timothy, who represented him in a difficult confrontation, and Titus, who carried his harsh letter of rebuke (BRUC, 273-274). Paul has proven himself in these three ways to be an ethical persuader.

FENCE #1: DO NO HARM.

Paul starts with the bare minimum. At the very least, pastors should do no harm. He says that he "wronged" (ἠδικήσαμεν) no one in Corinth. The verb was commonly used in the Septuagint to refer to sin against God; however, in the New Testament, it has lost much of that stronger meaning. The usage in the New Testament suggests general wrongdoing. When used with an object like a person, it often means to hurt someone (TDNT, 1:157-161). Pastors, at the very least, must not hurt people, hardly a high bar for ethics!

FENCE #2: LEAD NO ONE ASTRAY.

The verb (ἐφθείραμεν) generally means to corrupt or ruin with respect to morals, money, or doctrine (RIEN, 475). Paul uses the same word a few chapters later (2 Cor. 11:3) to warn the Corinthians that they could be "led astray" (φθαρῇ) by Satan "from the simplicity and purity of devotion to Christ." Paul also writes "Do not be deceived: Bad company corrupts (φθείρουσιν) good morals" (1 Cor. 15:33). He is warning believers not to keep company with those who deny the resurrection of the dead and promote sinful living (NIDNTT, 1:468-469). Pastors must be careful not to lead others astray morally or doctrinally.

FENCE #3: DON'T USE PEOPLE FOR PERSONAL GAIN.

The verb translated "took advantage of" (ἐπλεονεκτήσαμεν) literally means to have more of something. In the Greco-Roman world it meant a hunger for power or to seek political gain. The idea included treating others arrogantly. Paul uses it frequently to mean seeking material possessions by taking advantage of people. Paul even commanded that we avoid anyone who coveted possessions and placed coveteousness (πλεονέκτης) on par with sexual sin (1 Cor. 5:10-11). False prophets exploit people out of greed (πλεονεξία), leading to God's judgment (2 Peter 2:3). Paul warns pastors not to use flattery or greed (πλεονεξίας) because God examines our hearts (1 Thess. 2:4-5). A pastor must not cheat or defraud anyone. We must not abuse our power to get our way (TDNT, 6:266-274).

Effective pastors work within God's fences for healthy persuasion.

THE GLORY OF THE MINISTRY

In March of 1911, the Greek grammarian and preacher, A.T. Robertson, spoke at the Tabernacle Bible Conference in Atlanta, Georgia. He delivered a series of eight messages from 2 Corinthians 2:14-7:4 entitled *The Glory of the Ministry: Paul's Exultation in Preaching* which was later published in book form. Robertson spoke in his opening sermon of the discouragement that can overwhelm a pastor in the daily tensions of ministering to people. He wrote:

> *At such a time one is oversensitive and imagines all kinds of slights and insults. The real difficulties and problems of the ministry are magnified out of all proportion to the facts. In such a case a minister is in jeopardy. He is in danger of becoming bitter towards the world, jealous of other ministers, disgusted with his own task. Thus he will lose his compass and drift out to sea* (ATRG, pp.23-24).

In the last verse of Paul's grand parenthesis on the glory of the ministry, he wrote, *Great is my confidence in you; great is my boasting on your behalf. I am filled with comfort; I am overflowing with joy in all our affliction* (2 Cor. 7:4). Paul had been paralyzed by discouragement to the point that he couldn't even tackle the new ministry door God had opened for him (2 Cor. 2:12-13). Now he exults in the ministry, having received a good report about the church in Corinth. God had transformed his despair into exultation through people. What is the glory of ministry? The glory of ministry is people, warts and all, being changed by God's grace into Christ's image!

"I am filled with comfort," Paul writes. The verb translated "I am filled" (πεπλήρωμαι) is a perfect passive indicative. We can bring out the force of the perfect tense by translating it, "I have been filled with ongoing results!" The passive voice indicates that someone other than Paul filled him with comfort. We can't just talk ourselves out of discouragement by positive thinking. God has filled Paul with comfort by delivering good news about the Corinthian response to his letter. The word for "comfort" (παρακλήσει) can also mean encouragement (BAGD, 618). God encourages us in ministry through the encouragement of other Christians. We desperately need such encouragement many times in our lives as we serve the Lord.

"I am overflowing with joy," Paul continues. The word translated "I am overflowing" (ὑπερπερισσεύομαι) is in the present tense. Paul is continually overflowing with joy. The present tense indicates ongoing action in his life. The verb περισσεύω by itself means "to be present overabundantly." Paul adds the preposition ὑπερ to the verb περισσεύω, making it mean to be present super overabundantly! You can't get any more abundant than that! In financial terms, it means "to make over-rich!" (TDNT, 6:58-59) The wealthiest person in the world doesn't have more joy than Paul who is "over-rich" with joy because of the work of God in the people he loves.

However, we do not find our joy in the absence of affliction. We find our joy in the midst of affliction. The preposition ἐπὶ, which introduces the idea of affliction does not introduce a post-stress result. It should be translated "in" or "at" (MEY, 564). The pressure of ministry that Paul feels continues unabated. Paul now realizes that even in the depths of his discouragement God was "leading him in triumph in Christ" (2 Cor. 2:14). His exultation in seeing his stress from God's perspective led him to write his lengthy parenthesis on the glory of the ministry (2 Cor. 2:14-7:4). God is always leading us in triumph especially when we can't see Him at work in our circumstances.

We can be "over-rich" in exultation even in sacrificial service. We may not be wealthy in the rewards of this life, but we can be super-wealthy in the joys of the next one as long as we invest in people because people have eternal value. A.T. Robertson concluded his final message to the pastors with these words about Paul that remind us to exult in the ministry.

> *He had missed making money but had won the whole world. He had to the full all that was worth having, all that was enduring. He is the richest man in all the world as he writes the last words of this matchless panegyric on the Christian ministry* (ATRG, p.241).

2 CORINTHIANS 6:14-7:1

Stop being mismated with unbelievers
14 Μὴ γίνεσθε ἑτεροζυγοῦντες ἀπίστοις·

    For what common share has righteousness and darkness,
    τίς γὰρ μετοχὴ δικαιοσύνῃ καὶ ἀνομίᾳ,
    or what association has light with darkness?
    ἢ τίς κοινωνία φωτὶ πρὸς σκότος;
    and what agreement has Christ with Belial,
15 τίς δὲ συμφώνησις Χριστοῦ πρὸς Βελιάρ,
    Or what part does a believer share with an unbeliever?
    ἢ τίς μερὶς πιστῷ μετὰ ἀπίστου;
    or what joint decision has the temple of God with idols?
16 τίς δὲ συγκατάθεσις ναῷ θεοῦ μετὰ εἰδώλων;

        For we ourselves are the temple of the living God,
        ἡμεῖς γὰρ ναὸς θεοῦ ἐσμεν ζῶντος,

            just as God said that
            καθὼς εἶπεν ὁ θεὸς ὅτι

                I will be at home and walk among them
                ἐνοικήσω ἐν αὐτοῖς καὶ ἐμπεριπατήσω
                and I will be their God and they, themselves, will be my people.
                καὶ ἔσομαι αὐτῶν θεὸς καὶ αὐτοὶ ἔσονταί μου λαός.

Therefore
17 διὸ

        Come out from the middle of them
    ἐξέλθατε ἐκ μέσου αὐτῶν

        and be separate, says the Lord,
        καὶ ἀφορίσθητε, λέγει κύριος,
        and what is polluted do not touch
        καὶ ἀκαθάρτου μὴ ἅπτεσθε·
    and I in response will welcome you
    κἀγὼ εἰσδέξομαι ὑμᾶς

        and I will be to you for a father
        18 καὶ ἔσομαι ὑμῖν εἰς πατέρα
        And you yourselves will be to me for sons and daughters, says the Lord Almighty
        καὶ ὑμεῖς ἔσεσθέ μοι εἰς υἱοὺς καὶ θυγατέρας, λέγει κύριος παντοκράτωρ.
        These
        1 Ταύτας

Therefore
οὖν

        having the promises, beloved,
        ἔχοντες τὰς ἐπαγγελίας, ἀγαπητοί,
    Let us purify ourselves from every pollution of flesh and spirit,
    καθαρίσωμεν ἑαυτοὺς ἀπὸ παντὸς μολυσμοῦ σαρκὸς καὶ πνεύματος,
        accomplishing holiness in the fear of God.
        ἐπιτελοῦντες ἁγιωσύνην ἐν φόβῳ θεοῦ.

PREACHING POINTS

The central idea explains how we are to live with integrity for Christ. There are three preaching points. The first preaching point challenges us to avoid compromise. The second preaching point explains how separation from the world breeds fellowship with God. The third preaching point exhorts us to purify our lives for the Lord. The three preaching points form a progression of thought culminating in the final exhortation.

Central Idea:

1. (vs. 14-16)

2. (vs. 17-18)

3. (vs. 1)

Briefly identify two contemporary life parallels to these verses.

CLP #1

CLP #2

MISMATED IN MINISTRY

Christians must have wide-open hearts (2 Cor. 6:13) combined with single-minded devotion (2 Cor. 6:14). Paul qualifies his command to open their hearts with a second command to avoid becoming mismated in ministry. He writes, "Do not continue becoming mismated with faithless people (2 Cor. 6:14).

The verb "mismated" or "unequally yoked" (ἑτεροζυγοῦντες) is a present participle indicating ongoing activity. The present imperative "become" (γίνεσθε) when combined with the adversative "not" (μὴ) implies that the Christians need to stop something they are already doing (HUGH, p.245, fn6). Being mismated was most commonly used for draft animals that needed different yokes such as a donkey and an ox (BAGD, p.314). Paul was almost certainly thinking about the Old Testament laws regarding plowing or breeding with mismated animals (Deut. 22:10; Lev. 19:19). If they are unevenly yoked, the work will suffer (HUGH, p.244).

If we are unevenly yoked, our ministries will suffer. Some have argued that the word "faithless" (ἀπίστοις) should be understood as referring narrowly to Paul's opponents at Corinth and not broadly to non-Christians in general. However, Paul frequently used the word almost in a technical sense to refer to unbelievers (e.g., 1 Cor. 6:6; 7:12-15). Furthermore, if he was thinking of his opponents why did he not use the term later in his letter (2 Cor. 10-13) when he was specifically addressing them (MART, pp. 196-197)? I conclude that Paul is commanding us to avoid any entanglements with unbelievers that would compromise our service for Christ.

What practical matter is Paul addressing by this command? What is the contemporary life parallel to our day? He cannot mean that we should avoid all contact with non-Christians to live in our Christian cloisters (1 Cor. 5:10). The most common application in our day is that Paul is prohibiting the marriage of a Christian to a non-Christian. While this is certainly a legitimate application of the principle, it is unlikely that Paul was specifically addressing inter-marriage in this context. He goes on to discuss being the "temple of God" and not serving "idols" (2 Cor. 6:16-18). His supporting quotes are more appropriately understood as referring to pagan feasts in temples devoted to idol worship (WITH, p.405).

The Corinthian cultural context helps us frame some powerful parallels to our lives today. The political/social/economic structure of Corinthian life was the patron/client relationship. Wealthy patrons governed the economic, political, and social life of the city. The elite controlled life. A patron would take on clients who owed him for their jobs and position in society. If anyone wanted to be successful in the business world and enjoy the benefits of the social and political life of the city, he must pledge his loyalty to a patron. The patron would often host large dinners and other socio/political events to which the client would be invited. Every ambitious businessman desired to be included in these events so would pledge his allegiance to the patron.

Each patron would align himself with one of the gods or goddesses of the Greco-Roman pantheon as his patron god. Often the dinners were held in the temples devoted to these idols, so Christians were expected to participate in the worship of the patron's idol. The socio-political events were tinged by the imperial cult of Rome and the worship of the Roman emperor as well. Christians were pressured to compromise their faith to get ahead in life. Many Christians argued that idols were not real anyway, so what was the harm in participating in these social and political events. Couldn't they help Christians be successful, and so influence the pagan world? (CHOW, pp.104-125).

The best contemporary life parallels to this command revolve around the social, economic, and political pressures that can seduce us into compromising our faith in the pursuit of success. We must avoid any entanglement that leads us to minimize Christ's call on our lives. There must be no divided loyalties that would cause us to lose the consistency of our witness for the Lord. We must not trade our commitment to Christ for social, political and economic success in this world. If we do, we become mismated in our relationships.

PARTING COMPANY

The lure of success in this life seduces us into mismated relationships. Paul commands us not to become entangled with those who would sidetrack us from following Jesus (2 Cor. 6:14). He describes the entanglements that would lead us astray with five rhetorical questions in the following verses (14-16). Each question is a comparison clause governed by a different noun, but all five nouns combine to make the same point. We must part company with anyone who would sidetrack us from the direction Jesus has set for us in life lest we compromise our witness for Christ in this world.

1. Those who partake of what is right (δικαιοσύνη) do not share spiritual values in common with those who partake of lawlessness (ἀνομία), literally no (ἀ) law (νόμος). The noun translated partnership (μετοχή) means sharing, partaking, or participating. The verb form comes from two words meaning to have or possess (ἔχω) something with someone else (μετά). Paul uses the verb form in 1 Corinthians 10:17, 21 to teach us that Christians cannot share or participate in the Lord's Supper and also share or participate in the worship of idols (NIDNTT, 1:635-630). We must part company with unbelievers who try to use what we have in common to sidetrack us from our allegiance to Jesus.

2. Fellowship (κοινωνία) is frequently used in the New Testament to express the intimate bond that Christians have with one another because of our common bond with Christ. The root (κοινός) was used in secular Greek to identify a legal relationship of common ownership as opposed to private property. The verb (κοινωνέω) meant to share with someone something you have or to receive a share from someone who has what you don't have. The noun (κοινωνία) expressed a two-way form of participation either through giving or receiving (TDNT, 3:789-809). The idea is one of partnership and came to refer to the community of faith among Christians (Acts 2:42). Light and dark cannot share such a partnership because they are mutually exclusive.

3. What harmony has Christ with Belial (Satan)? The word "harmony" (συμφώνησις) means agreement with respect to settling accounts in a business transaction. A related noun (συμφωνία) was the name of a musical instrument, something like a bagpipe, and we get our word "symphony" from it. Matthew 20:13 uses the verb (συμφωνέω) for agreeing to the price of something (MM, pp.598-599). How can believers set a price tag on Christ in an attempt to barter a deal with the devil? Yet, sometimes Christians are tempted to trade the principles of our faith for financial success in the business world. Like Esau, we will sell our birthright in Christ for a pot of stew from the world.

4. What part does a believer have with an unbeliever? The word "part" (μερὶς) means a portion or share of something larger - a part of a whole. Luke uses it to describe the district of Macedonia, which is part of a larger Roman province (Acts 16:12). The word is also used of a share of grain stored in a room and a portion of land in a larger property (MM, p.398). A believer shares no portion of our eternal heritage or our kingdom cause with an unbeliever.

5. The temple of God has no agreement with idols. The word translated agreement (συγκατάθεσις) is only used here in the New Testament. It refers to a decision that a group arrives at together so often means approval or agreement (BAGD, p.773). The verb form (συγκατατίθημι) is used in secular Greek meaning "deposit together" from the idea that more than one person exercises an equal vote in a financial transaction (MM, p.609).

The list is climactic. The first four comparisons lead up to the fifth comparison, which leads into the quotations Paul uses in the following verses regarding spiritual separation from unbelievers. Paul is not talking about casual contact or missional involvement but separation from any relationships that control us in some way (WEBB, p. 163). Business contracts, employee agreements, political parties, and even patriotic fervor can pressure Christians to compromise their faith for worldly gain.

Lord, keep me from the worldly entanglements that would sidetrack my loyalty to you.

LIVING GOD OR DEAD IDOLS?

Idolatry in the church compromises the witness of Christians because idolatry pollutes our worship. The surest way to kill our witness is to allow idols to cloud our worship. Paul wrote, "Or what agreement has the temple of God with idols? Because we ourselves are the temple of the living God" (2 Cor. 6:16).

We think of idols as those little statues that people made and put in their homes or their sacred places. Those graven images were icons of something in the heart. The goddess of fertility was an icon for the desire to have children. Another idol was the god of wine and sex, an icon of the desire for pleasure apart from God. The god of power represented the power people wanted for themselves.

Americans are polytheists too. We build our spectacular temples to the icons of money, pleasure, and power.

An idol is someone, something or some desire that becomes more important than God.

The reason that idolatry must not be allowed to infiltrate the church is that we are the temple of the Living God. The better textual evidence reads "we are" (ἐσμεν) instead of "you are" (ἐστε) the temple. The "we" (ἡμεῖς) is emphatic because the pronoun doubles the verb and because it is first in the clause. The "living" (ζῶντος) God stresses the difference between the Christian God and the idols in the pagan temple, which the Corinthians frequented for social, economic, and business reasons. The idols of the world are dead. The God we worship is alive.

Temple (ναὸς) originally meant a dwelling place or home. However, it came to refer specifically to the dwelling place of a god in the ancient world. More specifically, the word was used for the inner sanctuary of the temple as opposed to the temple complex (τὸ ἱερόν) referring to the collection of buildings that made up the temple at Jerusalem (NIDNTT, 3:781). When Paul writes that we are the temple of the Living God, he is talking about the sanctuary where God resides. He cites Leviticus 26:12 and Ezekiel 37:27 in support. "I will live (ἐνοικήσω), and I will walk about (ἐμπεριπατήσω) among them" (cf. Jer. 31:31; HUGH, pp.253-254). God does not dwell in a house made of brick and stone. We are the home of God on earth.

When Paul writes that we are the temple of God, is he speaking corporately or individually? Is the temple of God the physical body of an individual believer (1 Cor. 6:19) or the church as a whole (1 Cor. 3:16)? Paul is primarily thinking about the corporate body of Christ, the church as opposed to individual Christians in this verse (MART, p.202; HUGH, p.252) for the following reasons. 1) The context is corporate. Paul is writing to the body as a whole - the church - not individual Christians in this chapter. 2) The pronouns are all plural pronouns. Paul writes that "we" (ἡμεῖς) are the temple. God lives and walks among "them" (αὐτοῖς). God will be "their" (αὐτῶν) God and "they" (αὐτοὶ) will be His people. 3) The imagery pictures God living and walking among the people who make up the corporate church. The pronoun can certainly be translated "among" (ἐν) which fits the sense of the passage.

Qumran, in Paul's day, had separated from the temple complex in Jerusalem to establish a spiritual community that worshiped God in purity and truth. They believed the priesthood had corrupted the temple worship. The community of Qumran was now the true sanctuary of God. Paul reflects this corporate sense when he thinks about the believing community among whom God resides. He lodges in our gathered assembly and walks among the believers who worship Him. We are His sanctuary, much like Qumran viewed their community as the sanctuary of God (NIDNTT, 3:783-784). Therefore, we must be separated from the idols of this world if we are to be the sanctuary of God in our worship. His presence among us in worship drives away all idols that might compete for our devotion instead of God.

The Old Testament Psalms picture the temple of God not so much as a place of ritual sacrifice and priestly functions but as a place where the presence of God fills the lives of those gathered (NIDNTT, 3:782-783). Believers long for the presence of God in the house of the Lord (Ps. 27:4). Believers cry out to God for help (Ps. 28:2) and worship God in His holy temple (Ps. 138:2). A temple is a place of spiritual comfort (Ps. 65:4) where God responds to our deepest needs (Ps. 18:6) and demonstrates His power to strengthen us (Ps. 29:9). So it is in our corporate worship as the temple of God on earth.

Western Christianity tends to be individualistic and miss the power of corporate worship. Corporate worship is the visible expression of the presence of God on earth. The sanctuary of God is not the building but the people. True worship is infectious as people see the presence of God in our gathered assembly. Our witness is most powerful when it rises out of our corporate worship. Our worship as a community drives our witness for Christ.

The presence of the Living God lodges within us and walks about among us in our gathered worship since we, the church, are the living, breathing house of God.

LINES OF LOYALTY

We Christians dare not compromise our faith by making unholy alliances with the idols of our culture. Idolatry tests loyalty. Paul writes, "Wherefore, come out from the middle of them and be separate, says the Lord. And don't touch what is unclean, and I will welcome you" (2 Cor. 6:17). There are three commands followed by a promise. The commands are 1) come out, 2) be separate, and 3) don't touch. The promise is a warm reception from God when we obey his demands for loyalty.

Paul cites the LXX version of Isaiah 52:11 to make his point. The final line comes from Ezekiel 20:34/41, where God promises to gather His people to Him when they leave the pagan world of idolatry (ARCH, pp.118-119). Paul draws a parallel between Christians in his day and Israel during the days of Isaiah and Ezekiel. The prophets picture a time when God restores His people after their years of living under the idolatrous systems of Assyria and Babylon. God proclaims the good news of God's salvation. "How lovely on the mountains are the feet of him who brings good news ... and says "Your God reigns" (Isaiah 52:7). In that day, they were to get out of the pagan world of idolatry without touching anything unclean because they were the carriers of God's holy vessels.

The Corinthian Christians lived under the Roman patronage system, which pressured ambitious believers to build alliances with influential idolaters in order to climb the social ladder of success (CHOW, pp.104-125). A businessman would align himself with a wealthy patron who controlled the contracts in his world. The wealthy patron was in turn aligned with a patron god and the temple devoted to that god. Maintaining membership in that temple cult was the key to success in the political and economic world of Corinth - the way to power and prestige. A businessman showed his loyalty by attending ceremonies related to birth, death, and marriage in the temple of the patron god of his business.

"Temples were the restaurants of antiquity" (WITH, p.188). The temples had dining rooms where the wealthy and powerful held their major social events. There were two stages to these feasts. The first stage was the "symposium," which combined a banquet with political speeches. Party loyalty was combined with pagan idolatry. The second stage was the "convivia," essentially a Roman drinking party (WITH, p.191ff). Participation in such events opened the door to success in Corinth, and many Christians were compromising their faith by pledging loyalty to the patron gods of politics and money to achieve affluence and influence.

Come out and be separated from such unholy alliances even if it costs your career! The verb "be separate" (ἀφορίσθητε) means to exclude or excommunicate one's self, but in the passive (as here) it can be translated "be separate" (BAGD, p.127). We are not even to touch (ἅπτεσθε) anything unclean. The verb can mean to eat anything unclean (BAGD, p.102) which fits the context of a feast. The word "unclean" (ἀκαθάρτου) refers to anything connected to idolatry because the idols pollute whatever they touch (BAGD, p.29). As Christians, we must not enter into any relationship which endangers our loyalty to Christ. The relationships may seem benign at first but later create a dependency that draws us away from our Lord.

God promises to welcome us when we avoid such alliances. The "and" (κἀγὼ) can be translated, "and I in turn" or "and I for my part" (BAGD, p.386). Our part is to obey Him. His part is to welcome us. The verb is future tense (εἰσδέξομαι) and means to take in, receive or welcome as a guest (BAGD, p.232). We must draw sharp lines of loyalty between the world's idols and our Lord. It may cost us to be true to Christ. We may face, financial, social, and political repercussions, but we must avoid any dependency on a party or person that supersedes Christ. When we maintain clear lines of loyalty to Christ, we will enjoy His warm welcome in life.

THE NECESSITY OF PURITY

The headlines screamed: Pastor Arrested in Prostitution Sting. A pastor of a church heavily involved in fighting human trafficking was arrested at a massage parlor using women who are victims of human trafficking. He was removed from ministry, but his immorality damaged the testimony of the church. Sin blows away our witness as the wind blows away the seeds of beauty in a flower, leaving an empty husk behind.

Purity is a necessity for ministry. We make a fatal mistake when we think that we can be successful in our service for Christ while pursuing impurity in our personal lives.

"Therefore, having these promises, beloved, let us cleanse ourselves from all defilement of flesh and spirit, perfecting holiness in the fear of God" (2 Cor. 7:1).

The present participle "having" (ἔχοντες) is best taken as a causal participle (BUR, p.170). The cause of our cleansing is the promises of God. Paul is referring back to the promises in 6:17-18 about God welcoming us and being a father to us. His loving promises motivate us to live pure lives. Paul uses the subjunctive "let us cleanse" (καθαρίσωμεν) to exhort other believers to join him in purifying their lives (BUR, p.74). Paul is not above the calling to purity. He, too, must cleanse his life of all impurity to maintain his integrity in ministry. The sad reality is that many of the biblical heroes of faith failed in the later stages of life and brought dishonor to God through impurity.

Christians should make a clean, hard break from all forms of compromise that might lead to impurity as Paul has argued at the end of chapter 6. 2 Corinthians 7:1 is the conclusion for the argument of 6:14-18 about spiritual compromise. The aorist tense of the verb adds to this sense of decisiveness (HUGH, p.258, fn 21), especially when combined with the preposition "from" (ἀπὸ) as in this case. Hebrews 9:14 uses the same combination to explain how Christ offered His blood "to cleanse" our "conscience from dead works" (καθαρίζειν ἀπὸ). Christ cleansed us positionally and called us to cleanse ourselves experientially. The preposition "from" (ἀπὸ) carries the sense of "off" or "away from" indicating that we must wash off the pollution of sin that contaminates our flesh and spirit (ATR, pp.577-578).

Writers have argued over the meaning of the clause "flesh and spirit" (σαρκὸς καὶ πνεύματος). Paul commonly uses these terms in a technical and theological manner. Flesh is human nature controlled by sin and is incapable of being purified until heaven. Spirit is the good side of Christians and does not need to be purified. These terms spark debate because of their technical theological meanings. However, I think Paul is using these terms nontechnically. He is talking about the outer and inner parts of a human. Paul uses a similar expression, "body and spirit" (τῷ σώματι καὶ τῷ πνεύματι), to refer to a whole person, both the inward and outward parts (1 Cor. 7:34, cf. 1 Cor. 5:3,5). I think Paul is using "flesh and spirit" in a similar nontechnical sense to refer to the totality of a human. All we are in our humanity needs purifying (MART, pp.209-210).

117

Maintaining our purity is necessary for effective ministry. We are "perfecting holiness" (ἐπιτελοῦντες ἁγιωσύνην) as we cleanse our activities. The verb means to bring about, complete, or accomplish our holiness (BAGD, p.302). Positionally we are holy. Experientially, we bring about our holiness by cleansing ourselves from all impurity in our human lives. It only takes one hard blow from a sinful choice to leave us with an ugly husk where once there was a beautiful flower of ministry.

Lord, keep me from blowing it all the way to the end of my life!

Made in the USA
Columbia, SC
14 August 2023

A Workbook for
Expository Preaching

Expository preaching exposes the ideas in the biblical unit of thought, so the sermon follows the flow of the passage. The hearers should be able to think their way through the passage after the sermon has been preached. The preacher seeks to visualize the flow of thought – to picture the structure of the passage. The sermon should expose the hinges on which the passage swings by developing an outline based on the structure but written in contemporary language. This workbook provides a structural diagram based on the Greek text side by side with a format for the expositor to develop an outline from the passage. Short, practical insights add exegetical depth and sermon seed thoughts to help the preacher flesh out the message. The workbook encourages the preacher to mine the riches of 2 Corinthians 2:14-7:4 for personal growth and sermon preparation.

David Christensen (Th.M, D.Min.) has served in dual ministry as a college professor and pastor for over thirty years. He is the retired pastor of Galilee Baptist Church and the President and Founder of The Rephidim Project, a ministry devoted to providing resources for Bible exposition. David is the author of four books including, "The Faces of Forgiveness: Healing for the Hurts We Feel." He and his wife, Janie, live in Maine and have two adult daughters.

The
REPHIDIM
Ex.17:12 **Project**

ISBN 9780578585727

900

9 780578 585727